MAN ABOUT TARN

Pete May

For Nicola, Lola, Nell and all Lake District walkers....

CONTENTS

ACKNOWLEDGMENTS

Thanks to my family, Nicola Baird for surviving the Coast to Coast walk and help and advice with this book, plus Lola May and Nell May for putting up with many wet climbs over the years. Also thanks to Steve Platt for the fell-running stories and Tom Wakeford for boathouse duties. The numerous people who run the Lakeland tourist industry also deserve much credit, as do the organisers of my 1976 Geography field trip. I'm also grateful to Steve Chamberlain for publishing my dry stone walling feature in the *Guardian* and Bill Williamson for publishing my tribute to Wainwright in *Midweek*. Thanks to Richard Boxall for the cover design and Kimi Gill for the author photo.

.

INTRODUCTION

Why get excited about the Lake District? Like most visitors I don't live there. I'm not even a northerner, just a soft southerner who puffs every time he scales a fell. My only qualification is a collection of Wainwright guides, some scuffed walking boots, a map case and a pair of walking poles.

I see the Lakes as a tourist, making two or three trips a year, sometimes solo, sometimes with my family. Walks on the fells are brief moments of muscle-straining glory followed by a pint of beer and dinner in a cosy pub and a train back home. My life as a sometime man about tarn began more than 40 years ago and still there's a desire to keep returning.

My visits have involved hail and gales on the Coast to Coast walk, soakings at Stickle Tarn, hungover hiking as a student, high ways to Helvellyn, mild camping, misbehaving dogs, children demanding pub dinners all the way round Wastwater, a try at dry stone walling, a lot of aches and many a sublime view. While there's nothing like a day of wind and rain to make you appreciate any kind of warmth and shelter.

I'm not the only person who chooses "Cumbria not Umbria", as my bag from Booths supermarket puts it. More than 18 million people visit the Lake District each year. Wastwater screes has regularly been voted Britain's best view. The Lake District is so popular that in 2017 Unesco made the Lake District a World Heritage site.

Not everyone agreed. In the *Guardian* George Monbiot wrote a column stating that World Heritage status would only validate the damage sheep farming has done. The Lake District was a land of, "wet deserts grazed down to turf and rock; erosion gullies from which piles of stones spill; woods in which no new trees have grown for 80 years, as every seedling has been nibbled out by sheep; dredged and canalised rivers, empty of wildlife, dangerous to the people living downstream; tracts of bare mountainside on which every spring is a silent one."

Monbiot is a great campaigning journalist, but the Lake District is much more than a scene of desolation. In private he's admitted to me that he enjoys dry stone walls too. Perhaps he has a point about the damage to trees done by sheep farming. Indeed, the region has been heavily influenced by humans. But in a way that has helped add to its unique charm.

As John Cleese in *The Life of Brian* might ask, what's the Lake District ever done for us? Well, without the Romans we certainly wouldn't have a road up on High Street, while the Neolithic Brits have left numerous standing stones. Without human activity we wouldn't have the dry stone walls that stretch up over the highest brows, the packhorse bridges, the corpse roads, the abandoned mines, the old slate cottages or the tiny churches. The lack of tree cover allows the sinuous curves of the huge mountains to appear, it adds to the beautiful desolation of huge rocks scattered over fellsides by the awesome power of glaciation. Massive scree slopes, hanging valleys and the trails of past glaciers are clearly visible. There's always a view from summits towards tarn (the name is derived from the Norse word for a mountain pool), lake or sea.

Perhaps Wordsworth and Wainwright, two towering figures of Cumbrian culture, can help us. Wordsworth had a good go at explaining what made the Lake District so special in his *Guide To the Lakes* written in 1810. He wrote of cottages made of stone and covered in lichen, which appeared to make the buildings half-organic. The poet argued that the relatively small scale of the lakes and tarns gave a much greater variety of shoreline and islands. The rivers and streams created infinite cascading waterfalls. He wrote that the water was clear compared to Switzerland and the still surface of the tarns and lakes gave wonderful scope for reflections of the mountains. And compared to the much larger Alps, every mountain was scalable.

Another great advocate for the Lake District was Alfred Wainwright. His seven guide books are extraordinary hand-written love letters to the Lakes. Every line drawing captured the beauty of the scenes AW wanted to remember in his old age. His 1980s TV appearances made him an unlikely icon, an incomer from Blackburn prone to bluff but profound poetical prose. He was also a bit of an anorak and his obsessive approach to peak-bagging encouraged the same tendency that turns many football fans into groundhoppers. His favourite expeditions have more recently been updated for the popular BBC series *Wainwright Walks* with Julia Bradbury, bringing yet more tourists to the Lakes.

There's also the quirkiness of the region to consider. The plastic-bag rustling habitués of youth hostel dormitories, the hotels and B & Bs with their strange English obsession for full breakfasts, the pubs with pints for sweat-stained hikers, and the people who trust you because you're a fellow walker and tell you their life story as you trudge across the fells. Plus the perils of following paths that disappear in mist and the rain that some days seems to never stop.

I've been lucky enough to see rainforest-covered peaks in the Solomon Islands, fly to the top of Mount Cook in New Zealand, take a terrifying cable car ride to the top of the Untersberg in Austria, see the jagged outlines of the Alps from Lake Geneva and spend time walking in the Scottish Highlands and north Wales. But there's something about the Lake District that still keeps me coming back. This is my story of how a Londoner and long-distance fellwalker came to love the Lakes.

Pete May

January 2018

1. ZEN AND THE ART OF MOUNTAIN GEAR MAINTENANCE

I t's the anticipation that is so enjoyable. In otherwise tedious desk diaries these days sparkle. A trip to the Lake District offers hope of escape to a purer world of rock, water, sky, pub dinners and pints. Thoughts will be clearer, problems less great. No more oyster cards, tubes, buses, cars and pavement crowds. While more importantly, a city man like me gets briefly to feel like a combination of Bear Grylls and Steve Backshall. The urban explorer can lie in bed listening to police sirens and dreaming about routes to a new peak while reading Wainwright guides.

Planning takes time. For a Londoner like myself this involves a lot of minutes on the National Rail Enquiries website looking at Virgin Trains timetables. There are big questions to consider. Is it best to arrive early in the hope of an afternoon on the fells, or late so you can get into Ambleside by ten pm after a day working? On the return journey should you go for the last train at 6.07 from Windermere or will that mean a wasted day if it rains?

There's always a huge array of fares and prices. Brian Cox could probably explain how we are all created from the stars and all matter is interrelated in less time than it takes to book an advance saver fare. After all that's negotiated there's the *frisson* of printing out your booking reference number, keying it into a vending machine at your local station and watching the machine whirr as several coupons for travel and seat reservations pop out.

As in Robert M Pirsig's philosophical tome *Zen and the Art of Motorcycle Maintenance* it's often necessary to avoid gumption traps and enter a suitably Zen zone of contemplation as you ponder what is the fundamental difference between good and truth on Trip Adviser, and what's available in Ambleside in August.

Finding accommodation is another massive Google search operation, performed weeks or months in advance, particularly if favoured haunts are booked up. It's best not to trust the reviews either as some folk are very picky. Website warriors fulminate over lack of parking spaces and kitchen spatulas. A cottage in Ambleside was lambasted for having a chipped cup and a cobweb in the cupboard. "That sounds just like our house!" quipped my wife, and we immediately took it. It was fine, very central, pet friendly and it was £200 a week cheaper than some upmarket rivals. A hardened fellwalker can live with a chipped cup.

Booking a room or cottage is followed by evenings of rummaging through the map shelf, then studying Ordnance Survey maps and planning routes, usually while my wife rolls her eyes. The green dotted lines that indicate a footpath always look relatively easy when viewed at night and accompanied by a pint of beer. But what looks a short walk on paper always proves much more challenging when you're there. Experience teaches the long-distance fellwalker to look for those tightly packed contour lines that denote huge chasms, lonely crags and exhilarating if scary ridge walks. It's always wise to have several possible routes planned. A low level alternative for when the clouds are low and the rain heaves down and a selection of higher treks for rare Lakeland days when there's perfect visibility.

Packing begins several days before my trip, as it's so easy to forget some vital piece of equipment. The first thing to pack at the bottom of my ageing Berghaus Dart daypack is my orange survival bag. My dad first introduced me to the concept of survival bags when he was walking the Pennine Way in the 1980s. Really they are just glorified giant plastic bags. But should you break an ankle or be stranded overnight on a mountain, getting inside one could save your life. It's waterproof and easy to spot for the mountain rescue services. I've thankfully never had to employ it, but it always feels good to have one as insurance should I or any member of my family be injured.

My survival bag has "Lifesystems" emblazoned on the front, which all makes it sound very technical, though it looks like it could be carrying your groceries from Sainsbury. It also has printed details of the international distress signal, which is six blasts of a whistle, or six shouts or six flashes of a torch, followed by a pause of one minute repeated several times. "If your signals are heard there should be an answering whistle of three blasts followed by a pause of one minute, repeated several times." Presumably if you only manage to flash your torch five times followed by a pause of 59 seconds, you get left to die.

My walking poles come next. These are a pair of Lexi poles purchased as a birthday present by my wife Nicola from the shop at the Wasdale Head Inn. They save a lot of stress on my knees going downhill and even when collapsed their handles stick out from my backpack, indicating to everyone else on the train that I am a serious walker. That is unless they are speared by them and lose an eye after a swift movement.

My waterproof plastic map case has a Velcro seal and holds an OS map folded to the correct section for each day's walking. Waterproof gear is essential too, so it's in with my Gore-Tex trousers and my Berghaus Gore-Tex jacket. Inside the zipped chest pocket are my compass, whistle and torch, ready to emit those life-saving blasts and flashes, plus an emergency hunk of Kendal Mint Cake. I've never known exactly how to take compass bearings, but stick to the general principle that the red arrow points to north so south must be opposite. When lost in mist and surrounded by a featureless tumble of rocks this technique was good enough to get me off Bowfell and back down the Band to Dungeon Ghyll. Generally though, I turn back if the weather looks appalling.

There's also my aluminium water canister purchased from Black's placed in one side pocket and in the other side-pocket the appropriate Wainwright guides and any extra OS Explorer maps, plus a folded-up photocopy of a circular walk from *Fellwalking with Wainwright*. A Tupperware container is added to my daypack containing some pre-bought victuals, such as Lidl's dried mango slices, some mixed nuts and Tunnock's caramel wafers.

Into my suitcase go my Zamberlan boots — the one thing you don't want to forget — with a plastic bag to place them in when muddy. If I've been pro-active they might even be freshly Nikwaxed. Then it's Craghopper trousers, fleece jumpers, two pairs of walking socks and other essentials like toothpaste and a notebook and pen.

Sometimes there is last-minute maintenance, such as buying a new plastic clasp to replace the broken one on my daypack, which makes me feel almost practical. Or washing my ageing Gore-Tex coat in Nikwax Tech Wash and then another round with TX.Direct wash-in waterproofing. I'm sure Mr Wainwright must have used something similar on his grey anorak.

On the eve of departure it's a good idea to check the Mountain Weather Information Service, which has lots of useful information on effects of wind buffeting and percentage likelihood of cloud-free summits.

Finally the urban fellwalker with backpack is on the train. Time to find your reserved seat, and as the train pulls away from Euston drink a celebratory Café Nero Americano. London is left behind and it's time to do some more planning and read some Wainwright guides for reviews of various mountains. Headspace is cleared. Soon it starts to feel properly northern as Wigan and Warrington arrive and then Preston, Lancaster, that glorious glimpse of the waters of Morecambe Bay, the strange graveyard of rusting old trains at Carnforth and then the shapely fells come into view as the train travellers catch glimpses of solitary farmers at work in lonely fields.

Passengers disembark at either Oxenholme or Penrith for the Lakes. The air feels fresher and has a cold bite to it as you step on to the platform. From Oxenholme, overlooking Kendal, there's a three-carriage local train to Windermere full of tourists and suitcases. At

Windermere station the first task is to buy tomorrow's lunch at Booth's supermarket and catch the open-top bus to Ambleside. From Penrith it's normally a bus or taxi to Threlkeld, Keswick or the shores of Ullswater.

Finally you've made it to the Lakes and then comes the idiosyncratic world of Lakeland B & Bs and hotels. Rooms come with a large variety of dodgy coffee sachets, biscuit packs and TVs with terrible reception. Yet there's something very relaxing about lying back watching a flickering Channel 4 as rain lashes against windowpanes.

You settle in to your room and place a few token shirts on hangers. How does the shower get beyond absolute zero and the sink plug come up? Will that shut drawer conceal the smell of your sweaty walking socks after a day spent trekking the fells?

The next morning hotels and B & Bs stuff you with huge full breakfasts that leave you immobile. People eat everything because their breakfast is included in the overnight price. Poached, scrambled or fried eggs? Hash browns? Excellent. Then there's the question of how to conceal the fact that I'm a non meat-eater from prying diners who have heard me ask for the veggie breakfast. Might as well print out a large sign saying "soft southerner from the metropolitan liberal elite." Is it easier just to go for eggs on toast?

If eating alone it's best to sit with a map and a Wainwright book so you look vaguely busy and walker-like as guests shuffle around the coffee pot and wait for self-service toast to appear while BBC News 24 plays on the TV.

Bald men in Lycra discuss cycle routes and weather

forecasts. "Today's meant to be a lot nicer — relatively!" Guests talk about pretty much everything; intrusive leylandii hedges, tracing their Irish roots or how they are a retired research scientist who once used lasers to study molecules. Finally, toast and fried food downed, extra coffee drunk, you sneak out with an apple from the fruit bowl which you plan to add to your packed lunch. The evening will see exhausted men and women covered in mud and sweat clamouring for pub dinners, cutlery in paper napkins and plenty of condiments.

You have arrived in planet Lakeland, home of Wordsworth and Wainwright, a strange English bubble that is saturated in coffee-making facilities, rain and wind. Soon the walking can begin. It's a ritual we love. But how did this rambler and unfit urban walker arrive in the Lakes? My personal *Prelude* began a long time ago in a county far away...

2. FIELD TRIP OF DREAMS

Spring 1976 — Autumn 1982

The Central Fells, the Southern Fells, the Eastern Fells

Bliss was it in that dawn to be alive, romping up to Stickle Tarn in a pair of high-leg Doctor Martens boots. The morning of Sunday April 25 1976 is my Cumbrian epiphany. For an Essex teenager on his A level Geography field trip, it's all a sublime shock. Where are the multi-storey car parks and flat fields of estuary Essex? Why is the grass so luminously green? At home it's a parched yellow, My world is Rod Stewart, Elton John, Mott the Hoople and trips to West Ham United, not dry stone walls and lofty peaks.

My home county is peopled by geezers driving done-up Ford Cortinas, with their names emblazoned in sun-strips stuck across the windscreen. My parents are tenant farmers who don't do holidays because they can't leave their cattle. You can see the Post Office tower on the horizon from my dad's fields and there are plans to build a motorway across his land. It's the last piece of green land before greater London. For most people in Brentwood the countryside means a country club with chicken in a basket and maybe a glimpse of a West Ham footballer. A trip to the mudflats of Southend down the A12 Arterial road or a hippy bonfire at Mersea Island is my Essex idea of adventure. But here are the biggest mountains I've ever seen.

We've been staying at a hotel in Grange-over-Sands. That morning our coach deposits twenty or so adolescent geographers, Essex *Inbetweeners,* at the New Dungeon Ghyll Hotel. And so we begin our epic climb up out of the Langdale valley. In charge is Geography teacher Mr Watts, a man armed with a backpack and a clipboard of facts about glaciation.

We pass through a gate ("remember to always shut gates!") in a dry stone wall and then travel relentlessly upwards over rocks that jar my oil, fat, acid, petrol and alkali resistant soles. Some of the other sixth formers have proper walking boots, but I'm sure my Doctor Martens will be good enough.

We stop to rest and see the New Dungeon Ghyll Hotel becoming ever smaller in the valley below. To our left we can hear the sound of water tumbling over boulders. The sun emerges from behind a bank of cloud and then there seems to be gleaming waterfalls all the way up Stickle Ghyll. Only why is it called a ghyll? For a 16-year-old it's a strange new world of clouds skimming over lofty mountains and stones crunching underfoot.

Scree slopes litter the sides of the fells, just like in our Geography textbooks. On we climb as sweat runs off my teenage forehead, and then suddenly the path became less steep and over the final set of rocks is a small dam and then the vast sweep of flat water that is Stickle Tarn. Half-submerged boulders lay scattered at its edges. Behind the tarn stands Pavey Ark, a huge glowering mass of rock, sheer black cliffs topping the lower levels of grass and scree. To the left is the outline of Harrison Stickle, looking rather like an upturned pudding. And in the distance stretch seemingly endless mountain ranges. Is this really England?

Mr Watts has short hair in an era of large sideburns. He gives us a short talk about the effect of snow freezing and forming a glacier. Expanding ice gouged out the depths of the tarn and squeezed down the valley like an abrasive tube of toothpaste. But most of us are more interested in our packed sandwiches.

Some of us take off our boots and socks and put our feet into the icy water of the tarn. A classmate declares that we should never do this as our feet will expand and we won't be able to get our boots back on. This is probably an urban myth, but we'd spent much of the previous month being terrorised about the dangers of the Lake District. "It's not a holiday," emphasised Mr Watts and the other geography teachers, again and again. They explain how the weather can change rapidly in April and we have to take waterproof clothing, drinking water and a hat and gloves and must definitely not wear jeans. Though Mr Watts never specifically mentions DMs, he does insist that we wear boots that support our ankles.

Sitting by Stickle Tarn I inspect my walking gear. It seems to be standing up reasonably well. My pale brown backpack is set upon a metal frame. An aluminium water canister is a strange new device purchased from Millets outdoor store in Brentwood High Street.

We've all been issued with black-spine Ordnance Survey maps of the whole Lake District, price 65p. It's a lot to get in to one map and it seems minute compared to those large-scale OS orange Explorer maps of today. But we get a general impression of the area and acquire a basic knowledge of contours. When the lines are crammed together it means a steep mountainside and the brown shading gives a 3D impression of real mountain ridges.

Once we have finished lunch our party moves on. Mr Watts leads us on to a path around Stickle Tarn and up over a ridge. He's right about the rain up north. A thin drizzle is now falling and I remove my all-in-one moped bodysuit from my backpack. It's bright blue and much too hot, even if it has worked on the A127. Today, I'd like to think that perhaps my appearance resembles Matt Damon in his spacesuit in *The Martian*, a bold explorer of rocky wastelands. Though back in 1976 my classmates seem to think it's more Michelin Man. Luckily no-one takes a photo.

Lagging back from the group of geographers, I'm stunned by the silence. Just the sound of the wind and rocks scuffing against boots. There's nothing like this in Brentwood, not even the Chariot chippie or Kelly's Records can compare. We descend a track and see Codale Tarn and Easedale Tarn below us. That's three tarns on our journey so far. We walk on feeling young and alive. There's clearly beauty in these isles way beyond Mister Byrite in Romford and the Southend Kursaal.

So this is what Wordsworth was on about. My English A level has a Lake District theme too, as it involves studying *The Prelude* by Wordsworth. Mrs Whitehead has done her best to instil in us the idea that Wordsworth saw a unity between God, man and nature. Though my pal Tim has already satirised the good bard with a piece called, "Growth in a poet's mind", which contains rather more sexual innuendo than in the original.

Still, I'm starting to see what Wordsworth meant when he wrote "fair seed-time had my soul" as he grew up with the sound of the River Derwent merging with his nurse's song.

It has to be said Wordsworth's childhood did involve quite a lot of recidivism. My fellow sixth-formers enjoy this. Within the first few pages of *The Prelude* William has already confessed to stealing game from other people's traps on the fells. A few lines later, after a trip to the village inn, he's stealing a boat from Patterdale and taking it out on to Ullswater, before being terrified by a large rock doing an impression of the Old Bill and provoking serious thoughts on his walk home.

Would Wordsworth have worn a moped suit like mine while feeling a blessing in the gentle breeze? If he had, the suit would probably have been from the helmet box of a moped he'd nicked one from round the back of the White Lion in Patterdale.

The rain ceases and we trek past the lonely shore of Easedale Tarn. Mr Watts gets very excited about glacial moraine, the giant boulder we pass, known as an erratic, and the rounded mounds of drumlins where the glacier has dumped its load. Stopping at a gap in a dry stone wall Mr Watts points out this as an example of human erosion. Behind his back someone knocks another stone off the top.

We walk down the valley, past more waterfalls at Sour Milk Gill and in to the village of Grasmere, which is bathed in the orange light of early evening. Our coach is waiting in Grasmere and on the way back to our hotel I feel for the first time the exultation of the spirit that arrives simply from being in the Lakes. The space, the clear air, the mountains with their mysterious gullies and crevices, the vast sky above. I've never been abroad with my parents and as my father is a tenant farmer, we only ever leave home for a few days a year to visit my aunt and uncle in Stoke-on-Trent. In my 16 years I have never seen anything like the Lake District.

Who's Next is playing on the coach cassette and the pounding synthesiser riff and Roger Daltrey hollering about fields and teenage wasteland on *Baba O'Riley* seems to sum up the sense of open space and all the hope and dreams that lie ahead of us. Then the coach driver put on the Beatles' *A Hard Day's Night* and the lyrics also seem to match our mood of youthful optimism.

We return to our hotel in Grange-over-Sands, which reminds me of *Fawlty Towers*. There's a fine view across Morecambe Bay. We're allowed to drink one light ale each at the hotel bar and then Mr Watts begins his debriefing session, telling us what we will need to write up back at school and then outlining what we will be doing the next day.

"Tomorrow we will be visiting Hawes..." announces Mr Watts. Suddenly there's an outbreak of teenage guffawing, ribald laughter and much slapping of thighs. It's the unreconstructed 1970s when political correctness is simply putting your cross in the right place on the ballot paper. Our party is mainly teenage boys. To our untutored ears it appears that Mr Watts is offering the stuff of sexual fantasy rather than a trip to an unfortunately-named small market town in the Yorkshire Dales. Mr Watts looks baffled. Eventually he regains control of the room and explains that Hawes is not a reference to prostitutes, but a place where we will view some limestone features.

Our seven-day field trip is split between the Lake District and the Yorkshire Dales. On the way to Hawes we visit Aysgarth Falls and admire the jointed limestone slabs with pervious cracks. Sixth-formers tramp over the limestone pavement on top of Malham Cove and note the disappearing stream, before travelling to the bottom of the Cove to admire the towering white cliff created by a faultline. Returning to the Lakes, the Shenfield School party views Ashness Bridge, which Mr Watts says is a famous viewpoint. We visit the toytown Bridge House over Stock Beck in Ambleside and complete an urban survey in Kendal. This seems to involve a lot of messing about in shops and noting down business names on clipboards.

We drink more light ale on the penultimate evening of our trip and watch Lindsay Anderson's public school satire *If* on the hotel TV. The film ends with all the teachers being machine-gunned. Luckily our only ready weapons are plastic map cases and sweaty walking socks.

Eventually that glorious week has to end and the coach rumbles back down to the south-east. My field report is written up and though I don't get a very good grade at A level a year later (I never really cracked human geography in Chile) the Lake District is not forgotten.

When it's time to fill in UCCA application forms for university, the University of Lancaster seems appealing because it's close to the Lake District. My other choices are northern too. Nobody actually visited universities before applying then, but somehow, in 1977, I'm accepted at Lancaster to study Politics and Economics, which is later changed to a major in English Literature.

As Lancaster is relatively close to the Lakes I assume I'll pop up there regularly, like Wordsworth with a narrow-lapelled jacket. But this is before encountering the intensity of student life and the rise of punk. The stone-built buildings of Lancaster do have a very northern feel though, and walking round campus you can see the hills all around.

In fresher's week there's an evening college coach trip to the shore of Windermere. Groups of students sit by the shore of the lake looking across to the Coniston ranges, asking each other what A levels they did and where they come from while enjoying legal pints in the Wateredge Inn.

There's a university hiking club with coach trips to the Lakes on Sundays. The only problem is that many concerts seem to happen on a Saturday night along with student parties, so away from parental guidance and with nine bars on campus the possibilities for hedonism seem invitingly great. So this means any walking has to be done with a hangover and sore Achilles tendons after a night pogoing to Elvis Costello, Ian Dury or the Jam.

I only make it to three or four of the Sunday hikes, though my diary does record that one Sunday in May 1978, after three pints in the New Inn the previous night, I walk up Scafell Pike with my pal Dave and that it's a "really good day out". I travel without a map and often forget the names of the fells I've climbed a few days later. There are no Wainwright wall charts. The Lake District is just an amorphous mass of really nice scenery that eases the spirits after too much ale the previous evening.

There's always a bearded third year at the front of the party who seems to know what he's doing who navigates for the whole party. So I just follow along and admire the snow that covers the upper fells. My footwear is still my trusty cherry red high-leg DMs, though I'm beginning to sense that despite their alkali resistant properties, they're perhaps not the best footwear for ice, unless you adhere to the Norman Wisdom school of mountaineering. It's a brilliant clear day on Scafell and we all return to the coach exhausted. Much to the amusement of my pal Dave a big bearded third year falls asleep on the seat next to me and rests his head on my shoulder, emitting loud snores.

During my second year my home is in Morecambe. After nights at the pub I wander along the seafront looking across the vista of Morecambe Bay at the silhouettes of the Lake District mountains in the distance. They gave a pleasing spiritual air to my yearnings for life, love, beer and a landlady who doesn't object to parties. But it's an hour's journey into the university and my Lakeland dreams remain largely unfulfilled.

Though my Romantic Literature essay on Wordsworth's ode *Intimations of Immortality* gets a first, one of the few times I've got up into the top echelons of academic marking. It's a great poem and the palpable sense of loss and passion for nature is not dissimilar to Elvis Costello or Paul Weller in its intensity.

In the summer of 1979 my thoughts on travel centre on an Inter-Rail trip around Europe with my uni mates Steve and Keith. I've never travelled abroad before and it all seems breathtakingly exotic as we take in Paris,

Munich, Valencia, Venice, Rome, Pompeii and the Greek islands. The provincial Lake District with its full English breakfasts seems a little prosaic by comparison.

By the third year, back on campus, it's time to study hard for finals. So somehow I've managed to get through university without climbing Helvellyn or Coniston Old Man, but having successfully seen the Stranglers, Blondie, the Ramones, the Jam, the Clash, the Boomtown Rats, Ian Dury, Elvis Costello, the Buzzcocks, Stiff Little Fingers and the Undertones.

My degree arrives the following summer, a gentlemanly 2:2 after just missing out on a 2:1, not that I'm bitter. That summer I find a room in Lancaster and take a bar job in Morecambe, mainly serving not very sober Glaswegians.

On a rare day off from the incessant pulling of pints my parents and younger sister visit and my dad drives us over Honister Pass. He enjoys testing his driving skills on the passing points, tight bends and tough gradients. We stop for my mum's obligatory flask of tea and on the way back snack on a new culinary invention, Planters dry roasted peanuts. Honister seems wild and desolate, scary but sublime, and I need to see more of it.

I leave my bar job after an argument about dodgy deductions from my pay packet. In September, while I'm still in-between jobs and renting in Lancaster, my mates Cris and Steve came up from Brentwood armed with a tent and ready for a Lakeland sojourn. We take the train to Windermere and find a camping spot in a field at Elterwater. The lumps in the turf are slightly ameliorated by several pints in the Britannia Inn.

The next day we resolve to climb up to Stickle Tarn

and the Langdale Pikes. It doesn't go to plan. The rain starts on the way up and never stops. My green Barbour-style jacket purchased in Brentwood proves utterly useless at keeping the moisture out. We're all soaked as we reach the lip of the tarn and gaze up at the glooming black hulk of a sodden Pavey Ark.

We wonder around the base of the tarn and pretty soon give up on our ambition to climb Harrison Stickle. So we find a flat piece of turf that looks slightly less inclined to pool water and set up our tent. It's an A-frame design, and holds up better than our sleeping bags, which even though in plastic bags, have succumbed to large damp patches where the rain penetrated our backpacks. It's more mild camping than wild camping. Though it is undeniably cosy in the tent as darkness falls, listening to the rain I wonder if the tent will stay put in the wind. Luckily I've placed boulders over the weakest-looking pegs to hold them in place.

Cris lights a candle in the tent, breaking numerous yet-to-be invented health and safety directives and threatening to immolate three loafers from Brentwood. Steve has a transistor radio and we listen to England beating Northern Ireland at Wembley. It's a strange sensation to hear the familiar tones of a football commentary in what seems like the windswept edge of civilisation. Someone lights a joint, but it doesn't have anything like the effect of laudanum on Samuel Coleridge, merely deadening the dampness at the bottom of my bag rather than lightening my consciousness.

It's an uneasy, damp night. Somehow we survive and stagger outside the tent to urinate in the grass and put on wet walking socks. We shuffle back down the path, defeated and sodden, to wait for opening time outside the New Dungeon Ghyll Hotel. When the doors part we console ourselves with pints of beer, huddling around the fire and attempting to dry soaked socks on the fireguard before getting on the bus back to Ambleside. We have been defeated only by the Lakes' elemental forces and a complete lack of planning.

My next job in Lancaster is a temporary position selling unwanted bespoke clothes in a Burton's menswear shop. When that job ends, I'm forced to sign on and endure a bleak period of unemployment back in Brentwood and Thatcher's Britain. By the summer of 1981 it's back to the Lakes with Cris in an attempt to do something useful with my dole time.

My dad had walked the Pennine Way just before retiring at 59 and has a lot of dire warnings about not underestimating the weather in November. He gives me his bright orange plastic survival bag, which I promise to take in case of emergency. Cris and myself take the coach to Manchester and then a train to Penrith, where we camp in a field by a roundabout before being awoken by inquisitive bovines.

The next day we travel to Pooley Bridge and walk along the shore of Ullswater before camping at Patterdale after a drink in the White Lion. Finally we take the bus to Keswick and illicitly camp by the shores of Derwent Water. The days have been beautiful and the leaves on the trees have turned autumnal brown. But still water and a clear moonlit night mean temperatures plunge more than we could have imagined. My new down-lined sleeping bag fails to keep me warm, so I get inside my orange survival bag. In the morning condensation has formed inside the plastic, making for another damp breakfast. It's as if my survival bag wants to drown me.

We're getting very good at guerrilla camping and walking round lakes but have yet to realise that what really excites most Lake District climbers is scaling mountains. Although that trip to the Lakes seems to improve my fortunes, for soon after I find a temporary job at the Housing Corporation and move to a rented room in Turnpike Lane in north London.

By the following summer of 1982 I'm living in West Kensington and unemployed again, "lying low waiting for the big one" as the sleeve notes of my Dexys Midnight Runners album put it. Perhaps inspired by my flatmate Julia, who is the most efficient woman in the cosmos and a great advocate of evening classes and self-improvement, I decide to use my enforced leisure time constructively and actually climb a mountain.

Helvellyn is, I erroneously believe, the tallest mountain in the Lake District. Having viewed the Helvellyn range from Grasmere, it's now the moment to scale it. For the first time I travel on my own to the Lakes.

Before my limited budget has been restricted to camping; now I'm booked into the luxury of the Grasmere youth hostel. Butharlyp Howe YHA is set back from the village and is a fine old stone building. The ambience is enjoyable. After walking up to Easedale Tarn on my first day, I find myself in the local pub with an Australian traveller and a Scottish folk singer. The plastic bag rustling of my fellow sleepers in the dormitories can be lived with. And so too can the fact that you have to perform a job before you leave, in my case mopping out the toilets.

This time I take my walking seriously. No more DMs. My dad has donated his old walking boots, which seem to have two-inch thick soles. It feels a little like walking with bricks attached to my soles. My new brown cagoule is a little better than previous waterproofs and I have a plastic map holder to keep off the rain. I even checked the route the previous evening.

After some initial doubts I find the path by the pub on the main road and set off on the long climb up Grisedale Hause. The steps upwards are relentless and my dad's boots weigh heavily on my soles. But I'm not alone. One of my musical heroes, Kevin Rowland of Dexy's Midnight Runners, also has problems with his soles, apparently.

People say hello as they pass you, which is very odd after London. The mirror-surface of Thirlmere looks impressive behind me. My training has consisted of pints of bitter and chips. But eventually I make it to Grisedale Tarn, a natural resting place where I can put down my day pack and eat my YHA packed lunch.

Then it's a confident trek up another very steep mountain, which is obviously Helvellyn. Only it isn't. It's Dollywagon Pike. Another descent and rise to what must be Helvellyn. Only it's Nethermost Pike. Another descent and another long rise with stinging thighs and finally and joyously I see the summit trig point. Staggering to the top I join the groups of walkers munching sandwiches and swilling water from aluminium canisters on the rocky plateau. And here is an amazing view right across the rocky bands of Striding Edge and Swirral Edge, standing above a vast blue lake called Red Tarn. The moment is immortalised on my Boots camera.

Walking alone there's the sense that the fells are a place to think through problems and reflect, or as Wainwright put it, "for a man trying to get a persistent worry out of his mind the top of Haystacks is a wonderful cure." My problems back home involve mainly finding romance and a job and perhaps one day getting paid for writing and whether West Ham would ever win the FA Cup again. But it's good to feel small wedged against the contours of these mountains, to simply concentrate on surviving the day and reaching a clear objective, such as a summit and a Marathon bar.

Retracing my steps back down puts added pressure on my knees and seems to last aeons, but that night I celebrate with a pint in Grasmere. The next day I'm too stiff to walk anywhere. Aching thighs, tight hamstrings, strained calves... finally I've made it as a fell walker.

3. MR WAINWRIGHT, I PRESUME

1982-1991

Alfred Wainwright is a very unlikely TV star. Yet in the 1980s he bestrides Sunday evening TV like a grey-anoraked colossus of the fells. Somehow *Wainwright's Lakeland* and *Wainwright's Coast to Coast Walk* becomes required viewing in the age of *Dallas* and *Dynasty*. Frankie Goes to Hollywood and U2 are on the pub jukeboxes, Margaret Thatcher is taking on the miners and Bob Geldof is telling us to "feed the world" with Band Aid. Yet somehow humble Alfred Wainwright, a man who hates being recognised, has gatecrashed the celebrity party, becoming both a TV star and coffee table bestseller.

The name Alfred Wainwright is as solid and northern as the man himself. AW, as he prefers to be known — he hates the name Alfred — grew up in Darwen, Lancashire. When he was 23, a visit to Windermere with his cousin and a view of the Lake District from Orrest Head changed his life, inspiring him to become a fanatical walker and eventually write his seven meticulous and stunningly illustrated guidebooks to the Lakeland fells. He also gave us guides to the Pennine Way and his own Coast to Coast Walk.

Wainwright is an anachronistic figure on my TV screen. Born in 1907, the septuagenarian paces the fells without a trace of Gore-Tex, clad in trademark grey anorak, baggy jumper, wire-framed glasses and flat cap.

The face of the former Kendal borough treasurer is framed by mutton chop sideburns. He puffs on a pipe while presenter Eric Robson tries to coax softly-spoken answers from him. He has never travelled abroad and has no desire to when the "earthly Paradise" of the Lakes lies before him.

What has finally enticed Alfred Wainwright blinking through his glasses into the limelight? His seven hand written, beautifully illustrated guidebooks to the Lakeland fells have won legions of admirers and a cult following. And now, sensing that his life is nearing its end, Wainwright has perhaps decided that if some southern idiot is going to make programmes about his work, he might as well co-operate and make sure they get it right.

It makes for brilliant television. At Kirkby Stephen, the sometimes curmudgeonly old soul mutters outside the Coast to Coast chip shop, "Fish and chips has been my staple diet for 60 years." The owner of the shop says he's an admirer of AW and his books are "works of art". Wainwright is beaming as he puts salt and vinegar on his lunch and then shuts up Robson's attempts at small talk with a brisk, "Let's start then!" He normally eschews the celebrity his guidebooks have brought him, and on TV looks positively embarrassed when he is spotted by a pair of elderly fans exclaiming: "Look dear, it's Mr Wainwright!"

Wainwright always seems to be on Sunday night TV when I visit my parents, now retired in a village near King's Lynn. In my mind he's always associated with my mum's sofa (the same design as Hyacinth Bucket's in *Keeping up Appearances,* much to my mum's irritation) and my dad's home brew.

The BBC2 shows begin with the gentle theme music and a shot of one of AW's immaculate line drawings and then numerous shots of Wainwright and Eric Robson pacing along rainy footpaths. Just before my dad retired from his tenant farm he walked the Pennine Way accompanied by AW's *Pennine Way Companion*, so I'm vaguely familiar with Wainwright's quirky tomes. My mum remarks that he seems such a nice old man and he really seems to love the mountains.

On the television screen AW enjoys reading the visitor's book at the White Swan in Danby Wiske, which he had criticised in his Coast to Coast guidebook for only serving him a packet of crisps. "Wainwright should come here now!" reads one entry from earlier in the day, noting that the lunches have improved. "He did!" writes AW, adding his signature in that distinctive script and sharing a chuckle with Eric Robson.

For the TV viewers of 1980s Britain, AW embodies a dour northern fogeyness that city dwellers secretly envy. In the avaricious London of 'big bang' deregulation and yuppies with brick-like mobile phones, Wainwright is a welcome diversion. His style of slow walking appeals in a changing world. He is often worried by "unfriendly bovines". AW likes to amble. He is undoubtedly a prodigious walker but he will always halt to take in the view, unlike the macho types who rush to summits without a break. And he advocates the joys of solitary walking: "If a man can't enjoy his own company imagine what effect he must have on others."

After the success of the Wainwright TV shows, a series of coffee table books are published. I purchase

Fellwalking With Wainwright, a guide to 18 of
Wainwright's favourite walks in Lakeland, accompanied
by Derry Brabb's evocative photography. It's a book to
dream with on winter nights. Perhaps one day I will
explore those shattered gullies, deserted valleys and airy
tops in more depth than during my Lancaster years.
Names like the Coledale Round and the Mosedale
Horseshoe promise much, day-long ridge walks taking in
numerous peaks. While AW's simple route maps and
descriptions make it all sound doable.

The Wainwright industry has begun and AW even
appears on Radio 4's *Desert Island Discs*, famously
announcing "next question!" when Sue Lawley delves
too deeply into his personal life.

In anticipation of future treks, my shelves now contain
several more of AW's guidebooks, purchased from
Stanford's bookshop in Covent Garden. He takes me in
to a world of varied ascents, ridge walks, watersheds,
contours and panoramic views. His bluff poetry inspires
with aphorisms such as the concluding lines to his
seventh and final guide book: "Always there will be the
lonely ridge, the dancing beck, the silent forest; always
there will be the exhilaration of the summits. These are
for the seeking, and those who seek and find while there
is yet time will be blessed both in mind and body."

Wainwright is a strange mix of old git and romantic
who soon joins my ranks of heroes sitting alongside
Billy Bragg, Elvis Costello and Billy Bonds. He doesn't
much like humans and donates all the profits from his
books to animal welfare charities. But the words
alongside the drawings display a mischievous side to
AW, a man who relishes, "pretty girls, fish and chips,

beer, ice cream. Yipee!" Sometimes a cartoon figure of an exhausted AW staggering up places like Kirk Fell appears in his drawings. Or a picture of a group of tourists looking for Blackpool Tower on the summit of Coniston while a solitary fellwalker sits well away from them.

AW uses words like 'habitations' and 'debouch' long before Will Self. He's also an early environmentalist, passionately against Ministry of Defence outrages and in his detestation of what the creation of Haweswater reservoir has done by submerging the village of Mardale.

Why has Wainwright spent every night for 13 years obsessively compiling his guidebooks? Today he might be thought to be "on the spectrum". He was dreadfully unhappy in his first marriage, initially too conventional to divorce and escaping to the fells whenever he could, climbing every fell by every possible route and then producing his stunning line drawings from photographs. Yet late in life he found love with his second wife Betty, wrote her long romantic letters and became a much happier man, even though she did make him cut down on the chips.

Meanwhile 1980s life has intervened between the Lakes and myself. I've spent two and a half years working in the press office of the National Dairy Council, followed by redundancy. But during that time I've been producing a fanzine, *Notes From Underground*, with my old school pal Paul, which gives both of us a taste for writing. After a few months of unemployment I finally break into journalism with a job on a listings magazine. After nine months I'm sacked, unjustly, and become a freelance journalist after winning a tribunal case claiming that my former employer had issued an untrue statement of dismissal. Suddenly I'm very busy looking for assignments and actually getting published in the likes of *City Limits* and *Midweek*.

Holidays have seen me skirt the Celtic fringes. There's a two-week solo rail trip around Scotland in the early eighties where I take in John O'Groats and Loch Ness. Plus visits to the Edinburgh Fringe Festival, a trip to Ireland with my old flatmate Sean and some coastal walking in Penzance, where my pal John has bought a cottage. There's a holiday in Skye with a group of rock climbers. It's all vast and stunning and with some puffing I scale several peaks with unpronounceable Gaelic names. This unfit Londoner even gets up to the Inaccessible Pinnacle on the Cuillin ridge. Only to decide it's very inaccessible to a man scared of heights and settle for a photo in the mist by its base.

In the brilliant comedy movie *Withnail and I*, Uncle Monty becomes over-passionate in his draughty Lakeland cottage, but that's as close as I get to Penrith. I watch *Withnail* alone at a cinema in Kensington High Street as Paul McGann and Richard E Grant go on holiday by mistake.

My journalism career has started to develop, though I've clearly fallen off the property ladder as prices race upwards. My 1980s rental sojourn has taken in Turnpike Lane, West Kensington, Hammersmith, Parsons Green, Fulham Broadway, Camberwell, Neasden and Westbourne Park.

Facing yet another eviction from a short-life flat I decide it's time to travel the world. So in 1989 journalism goes on hold and it's off to Australia for three months. Via hostels and coaches I climb Ayers Rock (now known by its Aboriginal name of Uluru), walk amid the bizarre orange and black-hooped mountains of Hidden Valley in Kununurra and fly in a light aircraft over the Bungle Bungle range.

Upon my return there's still the relentless struggle for work and accommodation. It doesn't help that I'm still a man without a partner, too poor and self-employed to get a mortgage. My attempts at relationships have been rather like my attempts at mountaineering; low level, poorly planned and frequently getting lost in mist near the summit, though with the odd vista when the clouds cleared.

Still, I'm getting some of the gear, and a little better than no idea. A bright red Gore-Tex coat has travelled with me around Scotland, Cornwall and Australia, and it has a torch, whistle and compass in the breast pocket. While sitting on the 18th floor of a Westbourne Park tower block in a short-life flat I feel a little guilty that my new Zamberlan boots have cost £70, while I'm supposed to be in dire housing need. They came with special Nikwax dubbin and it's a reassuring routine to rub the polish in after a trip away. My wardrobe also now contains a fleece jacket and some waterproof Gore-Tex trousers.

Then, early in 1991, Alfred Wainwright dies. It's like an old friend has fallen. The BBC screens one of his *Coast to Coast* programmes as a tribute. AW wants his ashes scattered on the summit of Haystacks, and I remember the words of his *Fellwanderer* memoir: "If you, dear reader, should get a bit of grit in your boot as you are crossing Haystacks in the years to come, please treat it with respect. It might be me."

By this time I'm freelancing regularly for *Midweek*, a free magazine for London commuters. As I've once climbed Helvellyn I'm deemed to be a Wainwright expert even though these days most of my time is spent scaling the bars around Tottenham Court Road. My two-page tribute is headlined, "You'll Never Walk Alone". It's the cover feature and has a front-page headline of "Peak Time Viewing". It almost sounds like I know what I'm writing about. My feature concludes: "We can only hope that the after-life is free of 'slutch' [a Lancashire word for mulchy mud] and that they still serve fell-walkers with beer, ice cream and fish and chips."

Having written about the man who loved the Lakes it's surely time for me to return. Though life will intervene again and it will be a few more years yet before this peripatetic budding hack makes a damp return to the tops.

4. 190 MILES WITHOUT A FLAT CAP

Spring 1997 — Autumn 1998

The Western Fells, the Central Fells, the Eastern Fells, the Far Eastern Fells

Hail lashes into our faces. Titanic winds threaten to blow us off the Straits of Riggindale. White mist swirls around us. We're into our 14th mile. I'm limping with a pulled muscle. And now Nicola is starting to cry. Tears run down her face behind rain-spattered glasses.

Wainwright's Coast to Coast had seemed a good idea when we started off from St Bees in bright sunlight. But suddenly the Lake District had produced a metaphorical boot to wrap round our heads. Never underestimate the weather. It isn't supposed to hail in May.

"Let's rest and sit down by this wall. We can always turn back. I've got a survival bag. And some Kendal Mint Cake," I mutter, hopelessly. I've met my equivalent of Wainwright's Betty. But I'm not sure if our relationship will survive our yomp to Kidsty Pike.

It's 1997 and much has happened in my peripatetic life. A short-life flat in a Westbourne Park has morphed into short-life flats in Victoria and Elephant and Castle followed by a move into Nicola's flat in Highbury. My career as a freelance journalist is going relatively well and in the era of Britpop, *Loaded* and *Fantasy Football* there are enough subbing shifts and football features to keep me in beer.

Some of the first half of the decade has been spent travelling. Entering my thirties and seemingly rejected by more women than there are Wainwright peaks, I returned to Australia and New Zealand, spending five months travelling alone and coming home via Thailand. It was a time of reflection. My sojourn takes in a flight to the top of Mount Cook, a cruise down Milford Sound observing the mile-high Mitre Peak, walks in the Queensland rain forest, Sydney Harbour bridge, bright blue volcanic lakes on islands off Koh Samui and quite possibly attack ships on fire off the shoulder of Orion. All enough to make me temporarily forget about boring old British travel and the Lake District.

My first encounter with Nicola is while sub-editing at the *New Statesman* as our eyes meet across a page proof. She's an environmentalist, recently returned from two years away as a Voluntary Service Overseas (VSO) worker in the Solomon Islands. She's temporarily fundraising for the editor Steve Platt to help cover the magazine's legal costs in a libel case brought by the Prime Minister John Major. Nicola's a keen urban cyclist. Her red Gore-Tex matches mine and is stained black from exhaust emissions. After a couple of months of chatting by the coffee percolator we start dating.

Immediately after we meet Nicola's temporary job ends and she moves to Oxford to be closer to the epicentre of the ten people who seemingly run the green movement. But I visit her at weekends and our relationship flourishes by the River Cherwell. We even get through a weekend in a cottage in Wales, which has no roof and Oxford greens discussing the 'tragedy of the commons' over breakfast. I guess we'll always have Powys.

A year later we move in to her flat in Highbury, London, which she owns. Just as long as the mortgage is paid we're safe from dodgy landlords. Our big summer trip in 1995 is to the Solomon Islands, where Nicola worked for VSO. The Solomons is a lot more humid and dangerous than the Lake District. We stay in a cave on Bellona and dodge a sea snake deposited by a bird and then meet menacing looking coconut crabs waving huge pincers that could crush all sorts of sensitive body parts. After slipping on a wet rock I even manage to fall into a water pool at the Mataniko Falls, but survive even if my camera doesn't.

Nicola is always planning weekends away and one of our trips in 1996 involves an impromptu visit to Lancaster where her green pal Tom lives. We drive in his jeep to his family boathouse on Ullswater. Tom's university lecturer dad bought the boathouse and accompanying field in the 1970s and planned to turn it into woodland. It's now teeming with vegetation and our first task is to take a scythe to the thick grass and vegetation. I feel a little like Levin in *Anna Karenina* experiencing the nobility of the humble serfs working in the fields. Our stay involves camping as his boathouse is damp and mosquito-ridden, but there's a camp fire and tea and sausages to be had and views of Wether Hill and the High Street range across the brown water.

I prove myself to be the world's most inept oarsman as we take Tom's rowing boat over to the yacht club on the far side of the lake, where his dad's yacht is moored. My knowledge of sailing only extends to Klingons on the starboard bow, but Tom seems to know what he's doing.

He takes us on a rapid trip down the lake to Glenridding, stopping at an idyllic grass headland for lunch and then sailing back just using the jib, which I think is impressive.

That weekend sparks a plan. Nicola and myself are both concerned about climate change and resolve to fly less, as it's the fastest growing source of greenhouse gas emissions. So we decide to do a proper Lakeland experience the following summer. It takes a lot of research and telephone work, but in May 1997 we start Wainwright's Coast to Coast Walk. Having completed his seven Lakeland guides AW invented his own walk across England, 190 miles from St Bees to Robin Hood's Bay and published another superb guidebook for it in 1972. It's familiar to me from the 1980s TV series.

The mainline train from Euston takes us to Carlisle and then we join a branch line down the Cumbrian coast, through Whitehaven and on to St Bees. This side of Cumbria feels particularly isolated, with the Lakeland fells and Morecambe Bay forming a barrier between the coastal towns and the rest of England. But although just eight miles north of the nuclear power plant of Sellafield, St Bees has a sleepy charm with a fine old private school, worthy of the about to be published Harry Potter.

Our guest house is homely and after Nicola chats to the landlady about the pictures of horses on the walls- —a useful lingua franca in country regions — we set off on our big adventure. Though first we send our backpacks ahead of us to Ennerdale with the very useful Coast to Coast luggage service.

We dip a toe in the Atlantic as Mr Wainwright advises

and take a photo beside the "Robin Hood's Bay 190 miles" sign. Our next move is to climb the path that stretches above impressive sandstone cliffs, some 300 feet above the breaking waves. Wainwright's route heads north over St Bees Head and then veers inland to Cleator. We pose for a photo behind a sign reading "permissive path", which sounds like something my parents fretted about in the 1960s.

A small stream gushes along AW's 'sylvan glade' of Nannycatch Gate, a delightful spot draped in bright May sunlight. Raven Crag rises ahead and we catch our first glimpse of the fells from Dent. We arrive at Ennerdale Bridge tired but exhilarated after 14 and three quarter miles.

Outside the pub a white-haired man sees our Wainwright *Coast to Coast* guide. "It's a lovely walk. Do it while you still can! Do it while you still can!" he enthuses, explaining that his legs aren't up to it anymore. That seems a sound philosophy and it soon becomes a feature of the walk that there are always people ready to dispense words of walking wisdom.

But just like our fell-philosopher, maybe my legs are not up to it either. My training regime of beer drinking and a weekly game of five-a-side hasn't quite prepared me for this. My thighs and calves ache and tingle the next morning while my feet feel close to blistering. But reaching the head of Ennerdale Water our spirits soar at seeing the vista of the High Stile range, Pillar, Great Gable and the Scafells overtopping a beautiful sheet of water.

The lower slopes of the High Stile range are covered in Forestry Commission pine trees — which Wainwright hates — but it's easy walking as we cross the River Liza and move up to the poetic Black Sail Youth Hostel. It's a former shepherd's bothy, a small stone oblong with a low roof nestling among giant rock-strewn peaks. The hostel appeared in the TV version of Wainwright's *Coast To Coast Walk*. Here the route takes us up to Haystacks, Wainwright's favourite mountain. It's a relatively low level peak at 1959 feet, but we can see why AW loved it so.

The top is a maze of weathered rocky outcrops and small tarns, a fine place to explore. Haystacks stands in the midst of a large Lakeland cathedral, with views of all the major peaks. Eventually we find Innominate Tarn, a small but lovely body of water with islands and reeds. It feels strangely emotional to be here, six years after Wainwright's ashes were scattered by the tarn. I check my boots for pieces of grit that might be the legendary fellwalker. Then Nicola takes a photo of me proudly holding Wainwright's *A Coast to Coast Walk* guidebook. Haystacks is the first official Wainwright peak of the walk. At last we're in Lakeland proper. There's clear air and just the sound of birds and our boots displacing stones. Twenty one years after my Geography field trip I'm almost a proper man of the fells.

We manage to get lost among a series of old quarry tracks heading to Honister Pass and spend ages looking for the ruin of Drum House. There's a desolate charm to the man-made devastation of these disused mine levels and spoil heaps. Slate gave a good living to the locals, who couldn't eat scenery.

Eventually we make it to the road. Here, seeing our backpacks and weary demeanour, a kindly motorist stops and offers us a lift down the hill to Seatoller. Nicola readily accepts, so there's still a mile of the Coast to Coast that we haven't completed by foot. At our hotel in Rosthwaite we feel a little better about our ethical lapse after a courgette bake and a beer. In the bar we come across a Land's End to John O'Groats walker who tells us not to worry, "It's not a race, you make up your own rules."

Day three of our walk sees us trying a Wainwright ridge walk, heading from Borrowdale on to the wild terrain of Grasmere Common and up over Calf Crag, Gibson Knott and Helm Crag into Grasmere. It starts off beautifully, but then ends up in a tale of gothic horror as a thunderstorm and flashes of lightning hit while we're on the ridge.

Nicola is convinced we are going to be incinerated.

"I'm scared! What do we do, Pete?"

"Erm... make ourselves small, I think."

"But you're a farmer's son, you should know."

"I know lightning killed seven of my dad's cows sheltering by a tree and he claimed it on his insurance. But not a lot beyond that. I guess we'll just have to walk through it."

I've never done lightning training with the NUJ, but I suggest crouching down as it gets nearer. Perhaps just our smoking Zamberlan boots will be found by the Mountain Rescue Service? If only I still had my trusty DM boots which would surely have been oil, fat, alkali, petrol, acid and lightning resistant. After a fearful trek across the rocks of Helm Crag, aka the Lion and the Lamb, we descend down into Grasmere relieved not to have been incinerated.

Here we have a rest day, joining the tourists to look round Wordsworth's Dove Cottage and discussing the holiday so far. The main themes so far seem to be the mounting expense of having to pay £70 a night for B & Bs, the lack of real coffee (a common trick at breakfast was to serve instant coffee in a silver pot), and the proliferation of Red Leicester cheese in sandwiches sold at sub-freezing temperatures. The relationship between god, humans and nature is probably in there somewhere too.

We set off optimistically for day four of the 'C2C', as a pair of Australian walkers we meet refer to it. It's going to be a long march from Grasmere to the Haweswater Hotel. The morning sees a trek up to Grisedale Tarn at the foot of Helvellyn and then, as a slow drizzle sets in, a long but beautiful path down Grisedale valley into Patterdale.

It's gratifying to see that the whole community has turned out for a funeral at the local church. Or so we think. "That'll be the BBC," says the pub landlord. "They're filming a series called *The Lakes* with John Simm." To think we came here to escape the media... what would Mr Wainwright make of it?

It's been ten and a half miles in the morning and we settle into the White Lion for a lunch of sandwiches served with coleslaw and crisps and a half a pint of bitter. It's a warm, pleasant pub and the cushioned benches feel remarkably comfortable after our morning trek. A Coast to Coast aficionado greets us with a cry of, "You're with Mr Wainwright are you?" He proffers advice on the merits of the high route versus the bad weather low route. The low route looks a much longer trek across Bampton Common and having had a taste of Haystacks I'm determined to see some more mountains. But the weather is worsening, I'm limping a little on my left leg and it's half past two. Nicola says the Haweswater Hotel, booked for tonight, is the one place she's really looking forward to staying and we have to get going quickly.

We head down the lane and on to the path up to Boredale Hause, a fairly moderate climb. But dark clouds are encroaching threateningly from the Helvellyn range, swallowing up whole valleys. As the path cuts around Angle Tarn Pikes the rain worsens and we haul on our waterproof trousers.

Cloud gathers over ominous drops. Angle Tarn looks lonely but impressive as dark mountains loom behind it. Luckily the path is well-furrowed here. On we march, past Satura Crag. Visibility is down to 30 yards. The winds rise, the rain is relentless. Ahead of us is another couple under sodden waterproofs. We stupidly follow them as the path fades.

We follow a dry stone wall downwards and past the ghostly form of a rusting iron gate, brown flakes covered in a glistening sheen. We head further down, hugging the wall, which offers a little shelter. Only it doesn't look right. The path isn't worn enough. There's a great deserted plateau below us. "We'll have to go back uphill and find the junction of the path," I sigh as wind buffets my Gore-Tex hood, pulled tight around my face. Every step uphill hurts. Keep my head down, look at my feet, don't look up, one step after another, come on, stickability. Eventually we find what appears to be the correct path. How could we have missed what now appears to be a motorway?

Briefly the clouds clear and we catch a catch a glimpse of Hayeswater reservoir from what I now know is the Straits of Riggindale. The path follows a dry stone wall, but the rain returns and suddenly the gusts threaten to blow us off our feet. My Gore-Tex hood is blown off my head and flaps violently. My waterproof-trousers are slowing my pace. I'm limping on my left leg. And then the hail starts, stinging into our faces. It's not meant to hail in sodding May. Wordsworth might have discovered God in the mountains, but up here we've found Him or Her with their washing machine on full-cycle and set to freezing.

Nicola can't see anything through her glasses. She keeps trying to prod me forwards as if I'm a horse. I tell her I have to rest for five minutes. She's not used to mountains and this is scary. I'm not very used to them either. We sit down by the dry stone wall seeking some shelter from the cruel winds. There are recriminations. We should have taken the low route. But that was miles too. We should never have attempted 20 mountainous miles in one day. And now we might be the first couple to die of exposure for the sake of a room deposit.

I try to think like Ernest Shackleton, telling her that a survival bag is in my backpack and that we can retrace our steps to Patterdale. She says we should still aim for Haweswater as we've paid for our room. And then I remember the emergency Kendal Mint Cake in the zip pocket of my Gore-Tex. Mint Cake got Hillary and Tenzing up Everest. It might get us to Haweswater. We both have a bite and the sugar kicks in. We plod on through a strange netherworld of wet cloud and precipitous drops on either side, if only we could see them.

We head relentlessly upwards, go round the looming bulge of the Knott and up until we find what we think is Kidsty Pike. The clouds clear a little and we can see a path heading downwards towards a lake, which must surely be Haweswater. It's just possible we might get out of this alive.

We descend into the remote Mardale valley, tired and battered as darkness edges in. When we eventually reach the rocky shore of the reservoir we turn left as Wainwright's guide suggests. A mile later we realise that this is the route to Shap and it would have been quicker to turn right and walk the four miles round the lake to the Haweswater Hotel. Nicola starts to cry again. I'm tempted to blub too. We slump down by a locked dry stone barn. We'll just have to keep going until we get to Burnbanks, where the dam is. It's a well-made path by the shore of the reservoir, but in the dusk it seems to go on forever. Lights from the hotel opposite taunt us with the prospect of shelter, warmth and dry beds. Are we going to have to sleep by a wall or break into a stone barn? We trudge on in the dusk.

When we finally arrive at Burnbanks there's few bungalows, originally built for the workers who built the dam. Then miraculously a red phone box appears, just like the one from *Local Hero*. It's dry inside. Shall we stay the night here? We have ten pence to place in the slot with shaking cold fingers and incredibly it's in working order. We dial the Haweswater Hotel and they kindly agree to come and pick us up. It's close to 10pm and we've walked 20 miles. Bloody Wainwright. It all seems so easy in his book.

But a few minutes later we're picked up by the Haweswater Hotel and suddenly we're in a warm building, running baths, taking off wet socks and then sitting in a warm bar. It's a 1930s municipal palace, built for water board officials. In the bar my windblown lips taste the best pint of bitter in recorded history. The landlady produces a hugely tasty Greek dish with an egg on top. It turns out we're the only guests.

We sit before a log fire as Ken the proprietor bemoans the southerners who want to know why they can't get mobile phone reception here, adding, "I tell them the cemeteries are full of people who thought they were indispensable."

On the walls of the bar are pictures of the old village of Mardale re-emerging from the reservoir during a drought. In his guide Wainwright is particularly scornful of the drowning of the village to service the taps of Manchester. There would have been a pub too and a much more convenient stopping off point for Coast to Coast walkers.

But the Haweswater Hotel is in a lovely secluded spot, alone on the reservoir. With the silhouettes of the High Street range dominating the view across the water, it all seems hauntingly beautiful after our near-saturated Gore-Tex experience. Both of us admit that some rash things might have been said as we yomped across the gale-strewn fells.

We cancel our next night's accommodation and rest up for another day at Haweswater. The sun is out again in the morning and suddenly this hidden valley looks incredible. After a late breakfast we watch a golden eagle flying from the crags of Kidsty Pike and then stay in reading and recovering. We're joined by a new guest, a bird-watcher, as we take our breakfast the next morning, and leave our Haweswater haven.

Refreshed, we resume our Coast to Coast sojourn, heading past the ruins of Shap Abbey and over the M6 by an ugly quarry, leaving the Lakes behind. But we see the waterfalls at Keld, the strange circular cairns of Nine Standards and at Kirkby Stephen find the very Coast to Coast fish and chip shop where Wainwright was filmed eating his lunch.

After reaching Richmond we return to London, but that autumn we resume the next stretch of the walk, crossing the Vale of Mowbray, then climbing up to the North York Moors, crunching through heather and gazing at the chemical works of Middlesbrough in the distance. The weathered rock formations of the Wainstones look superb in the orange light of dusk, as I walk on in my Philosophy Football Albert Camus green t-shirt. Then it's a trek along a disused railway line and the final glorious stretch into Robin Hood's Bay.

We've made it — all 190 miles. We dip our boots in the North Sea and then celebrate with a free half-pint of beer at the Robin Hood's Bay Hotel, where Wainwright had promised to buy a beer for every walker who completes the Coast to Coast. (It's now paid for by his estate.) Wainwright has become a friend over the walk and also briefly an enemy as the hail struck on Kidsty Pike; there's a much more playful air to his *Coast to Coast* guide, with his imprecations that it's not too late to turn back, symptomatic of his new found happiness with Betty.

We look at the black jet lying in the cliffs, and then take a bus to Whitby to stay at the Shepherd's Purse cafe. Fortified by all that outdoor air and some monkfish over dinner we conceive our first child. She dodges a Zamberlan boot really, as had she been born a boy she might have been christened Alfred, AW or even Mr Wainwright.

Our walk later inspires my 'Why I Love Wainwright' piece, which makes it into the *Guardian*. Rather presciently, 20 years before hipsters, it ends with the prediction: "I foresee the streets of Islington being full of men in glasses with mutton chop sideburns wearing flat caps, grey anoraks and walking boots while smoking pipes of Three Nuns tobacco. Wainwright chic is here."

The following May we return to the Haweswater Hotel — our last holiday without a child. Nicola is eight months pregnant. We hire bikes and Ken the landlord looks admiringly at the very pregnant Nicola, saying, "They'll be writing books about women like her."

While Nicola does a low-level walk I cycle to Mardale Head and complete one of Wainwright's circular walks. I've photocopied the chapter on High Street from his book *Fellwalking with Wainwright* to help with my route-finding.

It's a gloriously sunny day as I climb up the Rigg, the rocky spur that takes the walker past the lonely tarn of Blea Water and up to High Street. The summit's a level plateau but the path is clear and there's a historical thrill imagining Roman legions marching across this high-level motorway to Pooley Bridge. Wainwright's route then turns left to Mardale Ill Bell, over Nan Bield pass and up to the rusting fence posts on the summit of Harter

Fell. For all AW's criticism of Haweswater it still looks impressive from this height, while the views over to the Kentmere valley offer yet more promise of the deserted Lakeland the tourists rarely see. Indeed, I don't spot another walker all day.

Back at the hotel bar we sit looking at the mountains and then a sax starts playing, which seems ridiculously Hollywood. We later discover it's the odd-job man practising his playing by the lake.

It's a more restful stay than on the *Coast to Coast*. We cycle to Bampton and take a footpath up to Drybarrows where a pair of standing stones, one erect the other at half-tilt, gloriously frame Haweswater and the mountains above it. That's surely part of the attraction of Lakeland; the accumulated generations who have found something mystical about this area.

But our lives are changing. Parenthood beckons. Soon I will be a father and we'll be immersed in nappies and never have any free time again. Will we ever see the Lakes again?

5. YOU'LL NEVER WALK ALONE

Autumn 1998 — Summer 2002

The Northern Fells, the Western Fells, the Central Fells, the Southern Fells

Surprisingly, two months after becoming a dad I'm back in the Lakes. After enduring months of NCT classes (and frankly we could have done without the birthing pool video) it appeared we'd never do anything again except service our baby's needs. But Nicola is determined to keep working and not to succumb to the limitations of a patriarchal society. Her new book *The Estate We're In* is out. It's a green tome on tackling car culture and she's been asked to speak at a fringe meeting of the Labour Party conference in Blackpool.

We enter the hall at the same time as a breezy Tony Blair, who is dispensing smiles and handshakes. Luckily, the Prime Minister doesn't kiss baby Lola, bearing in mind my daughter's later Corbynista conversion. Nicola's fringe talk goes well as I change my baby's nappy on the floor of a cubicle in the gents — receiving advice and encouragement from men who are probably members of the Cabinet.

After the Blackpool conference is over, we head to Keswick for a few days, where we're staying at a B&B, which provides a cot. I'm soon carrying Lola on my chest in a Baby Bjorn sling as we walk around the autumnal trees of Derwent Water. The Baby Bjorn is quite similar to a backpack, but worn on your front. It has a pleasing array of buckles and straps and wouldn't look out of place in Black's.

Nicola says it will be good for me to get a walk in, so as part of my paternal leave I pace up Skiddaw, the great mountain that hangs above Keswick. After two months of constant attention to a baby and worrying about signs of colic, cot death and numerous other terrors, walking gives me a pleasing sense of stolen hours — a bit like bunking off work.

Cars scream past below the flyover over the dystopian tarmac of the A66, but from then on the tourist path to Skiddaw is peaceful and easy to follow. Walking by pine forests in the shadow of Latrigg and Lonscale and up past the tiny road with parking spaces until first Little Man and the then the airy summit is reached, with its shattered rocks and views right across Lakeland.

The area at the back of Skiddaw looks particularly enticing, with the lonely Skiddaw House set far below amid mysterious valleys, vast commons and elongated fells. I send a text to Nicola offering greetings from the summit. My first as a dad. And it's more satisfying for having a family to go home to. Now there are three of us. It needs some silence and calm at high altitude to take in what has happened in my life. But what was I doing wasting all that walking time before we had a child? Now it's a precious commodity.

Short trips to Cumbria become an annual or bi-annual expedition, all depending on an understanding partner. When daughter Lola is a year old I renew my Youth Hostel Association membership and plan to tour some of the Lakeland hostels — they're cheap and all you need is a sheet sleeping bag.

My train arrives at Penrith, followed by a half hour bus journey and a night at Keswick YHA, which pleasingly has a balcony overlooking the river. The dorms are not very youthful though. I'm joined by Terry and Bob, two retired teachers walking the Cumbria Way, who announce, "We're auditioning for *Last of the Summer Wine*!"

"We've been at this for 20 years. Whatever we're doing, every year we stop and have a week walking in July," says Bob, a balding man with a cheery face. "I think it was the best walk I've ever done today, I went up over the tops and Terry went through the valleys. You could see the Isle of Man as clear as anything. Now I'm afraid Terry snores, so you might not get much sleep tonight. But at least it's only one night, I've had it every night!"

"I've tried everything," says Terry, a chunky retired teacher daubing himself in anti-perspirant. "Sleeping on my back doesn't do it and I'm overweight which doesn't help. I'm afraid I've kept Bob awake all week."

After discussing various near-death experiences on the fells, Terry and Bob move on to Wainwright's books. "I don't think anyone will ever replace them," says Bob. "The towns might change, but the tops don't and you'll never better them."

Terry asks where I'm from. He shakes his head. "London, now that's one place I could never live."

"I don't suppose you can do much walking in London," says Brian, sympathetically.

In youth hostels these comments are as inevitable as

having someone sharing your dorm who snores or rustles a plastic bag.

"We do have some walks and it is easy to get out of London, It's only 15 minutes from my flat to King's Cross," I say diplomatically, retreating to the communal washroom where more men of retirement age discuss their days on the tops while applying shaving foam and cleaning teeth.

We settle down to sleep. Terry the teacher doesn't just snore, he sounds like he's about to take off. Aircraft tearing down the runway at Heathrow probably make less noise. Then there are two late-arrival Australians who turn out to be plastic bag shufflers. Had Motorhead been hostellers they might have recorded an album entitled, *No Sleep 'Till Borrowdale*.

But the smell of liniment, plastic cacophony, snores and early morning phone alarms can all be coped with fairly easily after having a baby. After nights spent breast-feeding (well, not me obviously) the soft murmur of the River Greta outside the YHA is bliss to a man often tormented by baby cries.

Next stop is Great Gable after leaving Keswick on the bus. Checking in at Borrowdale YHA, I take the bus to Honister Slate Mine, where Wainwright's approved route to Great Gable begins. It's always hard puffing up paths after a life of press launches and desk-sitting in London. But the rewards are great despite feeling terminally unfit on the old tramway to Drum House. I've photocopied the pages from *Fellwalking with Wainwright* and AW's diagram of the circular route is easy to follow. There are great views of the Buttermere fells and then across the long level stretch of Moses Trod the sight of the vast dome-like crag of Great Gable is unforgettable. It looks impossible to climb, but steering to the right, a path edges up from the walkers' crossroads of Beck Head.

It's a long trek upwards to the summit, but here I find lofty views of the Scafells, a stone shelter and a memorial to climbers who died in world war one. The view down the valley with a patchwork of fields seguing into Wastwater has me vowing to one day visit this most remote of regions in the Lakes. Then it's down via Green Gable, Brandreth and Grey Knotts (four Wainwright peaks in one walk) and back to the candlelit Yew Tree pub in Seatoller for a welcome pint and dinner with that lovely feeling of dried sweat on my forehead and a healthy ache in my legs.

The next day it's a yomp to the next hostel. For the first time I'm walking with all my gear on my back in a large rucksack, which makes me feel like a real man of the fells. My luggage is down to a few Fred Perry shirts, my waterproofs and toilet bag and it doesn't feel much different to carrying a daypack. My plan is to walk from Borrowdale YHA to Elterwater YHA via the Langdale Pikes and the bus from Dungeon Ghyll.

My walk retraces part of our Coast to Coast route up to Greenup Edge and head for High Raise, which is not much of a raise at all. This area behind the Langdale Pikes is a strange flat plateau at odds with the lumpy splendour of the pikes themselves.

The other plus of youth hostels is that you can pre-order a packed lunch. A cheese roll, an apple, a packet of crisps and a Snickers bar all taste a lot better when they are eaten sitting on top of your Gore-Tex and looking out across great lines of mountain ranges.

Then it's on to the top of Pavey Ark, where a group of women are discussing meetings, strategies and project management. It's striking how often people discuss work on the fells; it's probably because problems seem easier here, difficulties are placed in context, nothing seems quite so unsolvable. It turns out they're NHS workers doing the Everest Challenge, walking the height of Everest in 36 hours.

We chat some more on the summit of Harrison Stickle and then it's time to descend to Dungeon Ghyll and try to catch the bus to Elterwater. I don't make it, as descents always take longer than you think. There can be few more depressing feelings than seeing the last bus coming down the road while descending by Stickle Ghyll, then seeing the bus drive away while you are still desperately pacing a rocky track between dry stone walls. It's rather like listening on the radio to your team blow a draw by conceding a last minute penalty.

However, my spirits are raised by beer and lasagne at the Old Dungeon Ghyll Hotel. Not knowing there's a footpath by the river, I walk along the small road to Elterwater, which seems to take forever, but eventually I arrive at the hostel at 10pm, ready to collapse into my bunk.

After two hard days of walking it's time to rest-up and sit in the sun reading Nick Hornby's *About A Boy* by the old slate mines near Elterwater. As a soft southerner it's important to know your limits, not push your body too far.

That evening at the youth hostel all the guests who have opted for an evening meal sit down together in the dining room. Dinner costs £4.65, it's cheaper than the pub, and benefits from not being scampi and chips. But I also start to remember why my partner won't stay at youth hostels – they remind her too much of boarding school. All those plastic bowls for spoons, knives and forks, that uneasy shuffling over who pours the instant coffee and collects the soup dishes.

I'm seated with a computer studies lecturer from the Midlands called Kath, a grandmother called June with her six-year-old granddaughter Naomi and a Lancastrian cyclist called Bill from Arnside, who is perhaps the slowest speaking man in the world.

"I'm not sure I like being referred to as 'a short legged individual'," says Cath the lecturer, who's just been reading Wainwright about Easy Gully on Pavey Ark.

"He was a lovely man. I've met Mr Wainwright," announces June the grandmother.

"He were a funny old bugger," interjects Bill the cyclist.

"You've met Wainwright?" I exclaim in disbelief.

"Now let me see, it was 1960 and I was 30," continues June. "I wrote him a letter saying how much I enjoyed his books and he wrote back saying how he wanted me to be the treasurer of a wildlife sanctuary. Of course I said 'I can't do anything with figures and I couldn't possibly do that'. But you know what, he wrote back and invited myself and my father and mother up to stay with him in Kendal even though he'd never met us."

There's something touching in that gesture of inviting her parents; old Alfred always wanted to do things properly. June has other little intimate moments that make me believe her story — the way Betty called him

Red and how she finally accepted Wainwright's proposal on the weekend that they stayed. It feels like I've been almost close enough to smell AW's Three Nuns tobacco.

But on my final day it's back on the bus to the Langdale Pikes. They might only be 2000 feet high but they are instantly memorable to anyone who's looked across to their outlines from Windermere. This time I'm going straight up Pavey Ark via Jack's Rake. It's an exhilarating scramble across what appears to be a sheer cliff.

My Wainwright *Pictorial Guide to the Central Fells* has revealed the route, which cuts from right to left across the rock face. There's a small grassy ledge that stretches across the Ark. It involves a lot of hand holding and hoisting of legs and boots up eroded rocks set in red soil. As the Rake gets higher I gaze down at Stickle Tarn far below and reflect that any fall would probably prove fatal, but it doesn't feel too dangerous in good weather as there's a band of rock five feet wide to walk on. It has a lot of places where I have to stop and think about my next move, but nothing too insurmountable apart from one hairy slab of flat rockface, even if Wainwright says it is "as difficult as fellwalking gets." Slowly the top comes into view and after a final scramble it's out on to the liberating flat turf feeling very satisfied at my achievement.

If YouTube had existed back then, now would have been the time to post a video of my climb over some terrible 'inspirational' new age music. But in 1999 it's just very satisfying to sit looking out to a gleaming Windermere and across the Langdale valley.

Twenty-three years after first climbing to Stickle Tarn on my geography field trip I finally get to complete a tour of all four peaks of the Langdale Pikes. It's an adult playground up here, walking from summit to summit. From Pavey Ark to the memorable dome of Harrison Stickle, then on to Loft Crag and Pike o' Stickle, which has the air of some Tolkien-like fortress with big drops on three sides, an eyrie to watch over the valley below.

There's a continuity to this landscape. A great scree chute sprays rocks down into the depths below and it's here that the Neolithic Langdale axe factory was discovered in the 1930s. Ancient Lakelanders found a vein of greenstone suitable for making polished stone axes. They might have been more Neolithic bling than practical items, but they were certainly highly-prized, being found all over Britain and Ireland. The scree slope is now so eroded it's out of bounds to walkers, but here lots of stone flakes and axes have been found and also a man-made cave, a stone box that's six feet by five feet. Was it here that Neolithic axe-making folk stopped to shelter from the rain and eat their barbecued pork rolls with some cottage cheese and a Mars bar? Then it's back down via the steep drop of Dungeon Ghyll and the end of a great July break.

The following summer we book a family room at Ambleside YHA. We visit the World of Beatrix Potter in Bowness. While I'm paying at the till toddler Lola somehow detaches herself from her parents and makes a mad dash through the doors and up the ramp towards the road. It's one of those parental moments when your heart thumps and you rush out in abject terror. I manage to grab her just before she has reached the main road and raise my voice in panic; two-year-old Lola is very slow to forgive me, thinking that her bid for freedom is entirely understandable.

Once back inside the Potter venue we safely enjoy giant figures of Tom Kitten, Mrs Tiggywinkle and all those beautifully-realised creatures that came from Potter's love of Lakeland. Our friend Tom, who owns the boat house by Ullswater, has recently written a book, *Liaisons of Life*, pointing out that she was also a great botanist, brilliantly drawing and classifying plants. Her books are rightly celebrated but Potter was much more than just a writer for children.

Other years bring less successful mountaineering trips. If you've come so far and spent a lot of money on train fares and beds, there's always the temptation to walk whatever the weather. But it's no fun and sometimes dangerous going up in mist. Staying at Coniston Mines YHA one October, the spoil heaps, rusting machinery and general evidence of industrial trashing of the landscape certainly look evocative in the rain and mist. Imagine what it was like for the men and women who worked here through all weathers. But the zig-zagging tourist path up to the summit is soon lost in cloud and lashing rain and nothing is to be seen on top.

Scafell Pike is a similarly disappointing mass of white cloud and it's very easy to become disorientated on the summit. Men are often too full of testosterone to ask directions, but eschewing gender stereotypes I make sure to check with the next walker that my path is the correct one back to Borrowdale; the deep channel of Piers Ghyll looks dangerously inviting and is where a lot of walkers get into trouble.

On some rainy days it's best to try a low-level mountain. A midweek trip to High Close YHA allows me to explore Loughrigg Fell. It's a stubby little fell compared to its neighbours but has superb views of all the loftier peaks and terraces overlooking Grasmere and Rydal Water. The summit is a long flat top, which is a fine place to wander through bracken and up and down hills and myriad paths. Size isn't everything.

Working as a journalist the Lakes act as a kind of mental head cleaner — and it's certainly more effective than the head cleaner failing to deal with tracking issues on my VHS video recorder. It helps to get off the Apple Mac and just walk. Some wind and rain refreshes the brain, and I always return with fresh ideas.

In 2001 our second child Nell is born. My chances of getting to the Lakes are even more limited by parental commitments, but luckily Nicola agrees to a family holiday up north the following year. We rent a cottage in Torver, near Coniston, with our friends Carolyn and David and their daughter Corinna. As they come from Islington Carolyn and David bring their own cappuccino maker, which frankly we're rather grateful for.

The cottage is luxurious after youth hostels. Set into the hillside by the path to Coniston, it has a large fireplace downstairs, low-ceilings and cosy bedrooms. At the side is a raised patch of grass where and Carolyn and David's daughter Corinna, aged six, happily plays with four-year-old Lola. We're close to a stream, where the girls splash in Wellie boots among rounded stones and rushing water. We're close to two pubs, the Wilson Arms and Church House Inn, which to the delight of the children offer chips and pub dinners and a high-chair for one-year-old Nell.

We take the ferry across Coniston. Nicola tells us it was used as the basis for Arthur Ransome's *Swallow and Amazons*, a book that has a somewhat liberal attitude to health and safety but is loved by our daughters. We tell the girls, busy eating Magnum ice creams on the ferry, that, "only duffers drown."

On the other shore is John Ruskin's home of Brantwood, an imposing white building that dominates the shoreline. Ruskin was born in 1819 and became an all-round literary/artistic geezer, being an art critic, writer, social reformer and champion of the Pre-Raphaelite movement. The house is full of Ruskin's paintings and period furniture, while my purchase of his book *Unto This Last* from the museum shop reveals a fine Victorian critique of political economy.

That's all very well, but what lingers in my memory is Nicola repeating the story that Ruskin was rendered impotent upon discovering that his wife Effie Gray had pubic hair, unlike the classical sculptures. Which all seems rather strange in gritty Cumbria, where sheep are breeding and earthy procreation is never far away. The pubic hair story might be a myth, but Effie Gray did sue for divorce on the grounds of impotence, Ruskin presumably not realising that you could find lead for your pencil at the Derwent Pencil Museum in Keswick.

So here we are, discussing pubic hair over tea and carrot cake as we sit in the very English Brantwood café, overlooking the lake and a splendid prospect of the Coniston fells. It would have been hard for Ruskin not to feel inspired at Brantwood, where he spent the final 28 years of his life. Even if he might have benefitted from perusing some under-the-counter mags in the Coniston newsagents for basic biology lessons.

Coniston has many attractions. We find a local agricultural show where the girls get to hold border terriers and admire a variety of sticks with sheep horn handles. A farmer tells us that sheep fleeces are now selling for less than the price of a packet of crisps.

We go into town for some pints of Bluebird bitter, named after Donald Campbell's speed boat in which he tried to break the water speed record by travelling at 300mph. The grainy black and white news image of his jet-like craft somersaulting in the air and plunging into the depths of Coniston Water was ingrained from my childhood. Bluebird was finally salvaged in 2001 and Campbell's remains buried in Hawkshead.

Before we leave Lola and Corinna set up a lemonade stall by the footpath next to our cottage. They make a sign offering plastic cups of lemonade at 50p a time and even manage to make a couple of sales to exhausted walkers. This probably contravenes some ancient bylaw and they don't have a licence, but with such entrepreneurial acumen they may end up on *The Apprentice.*

We even get to do some walking. Nicola and Carolyn climb Coniston while we have the kids and the next day David and I climb up to Dow Crag and on to Coniston Old Man. It's reassuring that David is a doctor, as I'm again feeling terminally unfit after too many media lunches. But soon we get into the pace and discover that the path from Goat's Water up to Dow Crag is covered in huge white sacks of boulders, as if deposited by a giant with a bad litter habit. It turns out they've been dropped be helicopter and are going to be used to rebuild the path — part of the conservation work the tourist doesn't always see. It's an enjoyable scramble up Easy Gully and then an airy promenade to Coniston Old Man, Brim Fell and the angular top of Swirl How.

There are more solo trips in later years. Sometimes I bring back presents for the children, such as a lump of sheep's wool from a fence, a piece of white quartz from the fells, bits of heather or a wooden pencil case and set of Lakeland pencils from the Derwent Pencil Museum in Keswick. The museum really is an excellent place to wander around on a rainy day. Any building with a giant pencil outside its doors has to be worth a look. Inside it's very informative about just what a vital role graphite mining played in the region. Pencils were even the chosen writing instrument of astronauts, the displays inform me.

Other things change in our lives. In December 2005 Nicola and I get married in a homespun ceremony at the local church, followed by a reception at the Islington Ecology Centre. My mum has been diagnosed with Alzheimer's Disease and we want her to remember something of our day. The children are keen on being bridesmaids too. Strangely I can't persuade my new wife to visit Keswick or Kendal for our honeymoon so we Eurostar it to Lille instead.

But as a newly-respectable married man my annual trips up north continue, usually in the spring or summer. On our first wedding anniversary we stay the weekend in Keswick. But Keswick in December is on something like its 27th day of successive rain and so we stay in our room or shelter in restaurants. Another trip to Ambleside YHA is more successful. The girls are excited to discover four bunks in our family room and Marmite and hash browns for breakfast. It's a friendly place. Hearing our worries about buying walking boots for rapidly-growing children's feet, one dad immediately offers us his son's boots, which the boy has outgrown.

I'm not someone who visits the Lake District because I hate London. The capital is a source of endless fascination, with its ever-changing villages and skylines and the buzz of culture everywhere. While researching my family tree I've discovered deep London roots on my father's side, right back to a saddler in Commercial Road and a waterman on the Thames. But the Lakes are always an antidote to London overload. In the mountains the values of the media world and the rejections from 12-year-old editors and my spiked book proposals don't seem so important. My duties as a dad and the searching for book bags and hair clips can end for a while. The jostling and the pollution stops, traffic ceases to roar and perspective is found. It's a habit it's now hard to break.

6. IS SKIDDAW BIGGER THAN EVEREST?

Spring 2007

The Northern Fells

Walk anywhere in the Lake District and you'll see children, either having fun or reluctantly trailing behind their parents. Nicola thinks it's important to talk to children on the fells, to ask how they are enjoying it, because you have to make it fun and they need encouragement. Sometimes kids will need enticing with sweets and snack breaks or a pep talk. They will race up a slope and then collapse exhausted. Teenagers might just sulk and rage at the stupidity of it all. You can't turn it into a route march. But it's still a moment of family history when you take your child up their first mountain.

We're staying at Tom's house in Penrith (he's moved here to be closer to his boathouse on Ullswater) when I take my youngest daughter Nell for her first proper mountain walk. Eight-year-old Lola has been sick in the night and then up with diarrhoea all morning at our borrowed home. So she's been left with her mum and six-year-old Nell has Dad all to herself on the bus from Penrith to Keswick.

Nell has asthma so we have to take her blue inhaler with us, but we've always tried to encourage her to be active. She's benefitting from being away from the air pollution of London and if there are any problems we will turn back.

"If we go up Everest Lola can have chocolate, I can have my asthma pump and mummy and daddy can have oxygen," declares Nell, finalising our arrangements should we enter the death zone. I've just been explaining that you need oxygen for Everest and that here in the Lake District oxygen won't be necessary for climbing Skiddaw. Just a packed lunch and some Kendal Mint Cake.

"Is Skiddaw as tall as Everest?" she asks.

"Well, no, but it is the fourth tallest mountain in the Lake District at 3053 feet. Everest is a bit bigger at 29,029 feet. But for you it is like Everest, because it's the first mountain you'll ever have climbed."

Skiddaw is the choice for our ascent of a Lakeland peak because it's walking distance from Keswick. It might not be on the border of Nepal and Tibet, or indeed be the highest mountain in the world, but it is serviced by a path that is wide and easy to follow, the grey stone-strewn path created by generations of boots trudging their way ever upwards to the summit. Mr A Wainwright might scoff at such a heavily blazed route, but for a parent and child it's an ideal introduction to peak-time viewing.

We walk through Keswick's array of trekking shops and buy a coffee at the bakery and a piece of lemon cake for Nell. She already has a clear consumerist view from Skiddaw's summit. "Are there models of Skiddaw? Can we buy a glass boat with a model inside and when it rains it snows? And I want Skiddaw sweets too!"

We walk past the old station, our boots brushing

through fallen leaves, towards the main path to Skiddaw. Yesterday there was a Lake District deluge, today there's just the prospect of intermittent drizzle and we're swaddled in Gore-Tex, hats and gloves. The path begins as a track where Nell, in her pink fleece, counts fields. "That's nine sheep fields and one cow field!" We sit on a dry stone wall. Nell asks why there isn't any cement in the wall, and I explain the principles of dry stone walling as we catch our first view of Skiddaw and Skiddaw Little Man.

It's my hope that the promise of fruit gums will keep her heading upwards as she asks "Daddy can I have another gelatine please?" A bridge takes us over the busy A66 and Nell, just like her absent mum, shouts at the cars. "We have to stop climate change, don't they know what it's like to be a polar bear?"

Once the motorway is crossed it feels like real countryside. In the dip stands a pond with ducks and a delighted Nell declares, "It's a beach! Look! A duck shouted at me!" The cottages by the track contain free-range hens and Nell, of course, wants one.

Then it's the path proper, a steady upwards climb over a root and stone encrusted path through Latrigg Woods. As we ascend it's necessary to shed a few layers. Nell decides she wants to wear my red Gore-Tex and is delighted that it takes on the proportions of a cloak. Just as they do with adults, the mountains create a mood of contemplation. Without the distractions of our complete nuclear family it's a chance for Nell to confide the fears of her young life.

"Daddy, I want to learn to be a grown up. They can carry heavy things and not be shy and be good at school and help everyone."

We hear cries of "Excuse me!" as several cyclists zoom past us, their mud-encrusted posteriors jerking their way over roots and rocks as they judder at some velocity towards the valley.

We stop for a snack break at the first viewpoint over Keswick sitting down on my orange survival bag. We discuss camping spots and she asks if I have packed two pillows in case we get stuck. For the first time we see the full stretch of Derwent Water beneath us, the mass of crags along Lakeland beyond and a glimpse of Lake Bassenthwaite to our right. "Those houses look like doll's houses," says Nell, looking at the town, and I'm proud that it's the first time in her life she's seen a town from such a perspective. Then come more illicit snacks. "Mummy will never know we had crisps!"

Refuelled, we march up the path, reading a sign with a map of the pine woods, with details of the wild boar that once foraged here. The wood is dark, scattered with needles, but we find cones to take home for the rest of the family. And at the path's edge there are numerous fungi, including the fairytale red of the lethal flyagaric. Cyclists speed past us. As we stop for a photo a woman hiker sees Nell in my red Gore-Tex and says, "She'll win a prize for the best photo of Little Red Riding Hood."

We pass a section of clear-felled forest, a stream with mini-waterfalls and then cross Gale Road (where there's a car park for walkers wanting to make the climb a little easier) into a field of sheep and take the zig zag path up to Skiddaw Little Man.

Maybe we shouldn't go any further, but Nell wants to

get to the summit. We stop for an orange by the memorial to three shepherds from the Hawell family of Lonscale, a white cross that bears the apt inscription: "Great Shepherd of thy heavenly flock, these men have left our gill. Their feet were on the living rock, Oh guide and bless them still."

There's cloud shrouding the summits above us. It's going to take another two hours to get back down to Keswick. And then the drizzle worsens and the wind drives the rain into our faces. "Daddy, we're going down!" announces Nell, sensibly aware of how small humans are in this environment. We've made it half way up Everest and that's an achievement for a six-year-old. So we descend back through the stile across the road, and down the path back to Keswick, sheltering in the shadow of Latrigg.

"Let's pretend to be a bike!" declares Nell, "Run daddy, run!" And so we become human bicycles, clattering down the rocks, holding hands. "Oh my giddy aunt!" I declare, remembering Patrick Troughton's catchphrase from *Doctor Who*. Nell laughs with the freedom only children know. "Come on daddy, stand up straight. It's good for your muscles!" I've discovered my own mini-personal trainer.

Nell says she'd like to take an aeroplane up Skiddaw. I point out it might not be good for climate change. Luckily our chickens back in London provide inspiration for Nell. "We could fly up on Violet and Romana." Yes, we could become fowl-flying super heroes swooping over Skiddaw.

And finally we're back in warm and inviting Keswick, ready for one final treat from the newsagents, a bar of chocolate covered Kendal Mint Cake. On the packet it reads "Romney's Kendal Mint Cake was carried to the summit of Mount Everest by Sir Edmund Hillary and Tenzing Norgay on the 29th May 1953." And there's a quote: "We sat on the snow and looked at the country far below us… we nibbled Kendal Mint Cake."

Having covered five miles and scaled half of Skiddaw without Sherpas or oxygen we feel we deserve some Mint Cake too. It's my daughter's first half-mountain. We can't force our children to like what we do, but if she ends up with some appreciation of mountain country like this, then I'll feel I've been a half-decent dad. Skiddaw was our Everest today. And in a few years we'll be back to conquer the summit without oxygen.

7. AROUND THE LAKES WITHOUT A PLANE

Summer 2007

The Northern Fells, the North Western Fells, the Eastern Fells, the Far Eastern Fells

Nicola decides that our family will be going on a grand tour of Britain. We're going to save carbon and prove that you don't need to fly abroad to holiday. I'm happy to go along with this, and as my wife is a latter-day combination of Mary Wollstonecraft and Rachel Carson, she's unlikely to be deterred by my worries about seeking permission to take the kids out of school six weeks early.

Our lives are changing. Sadly my mum has died at the age of 79 after complications following a burst stomach ulcer. Her Alzheimer's was getting worse. It's a cruel disease and in a way it's merciful that she has departed while still knowing the names of her children and grandchildren.

My dad has been left bereft in Norfolk, where we try to visit as often as we can. On our summer tour of Britain we ring most nights to check he's ok. We're all getting older and there's a sense that life can't wait while we get trapped by deadlines and school runs.

Nicola's left Friends of the Earth to go freelance and has created a blog called *Around Britain Without a Plane*, in which we're going to chronicle our three-month staycation in Britain. We're both working freelance so can be fairly flexible. We present a plan to the education authority on how we will home educate our daughters as we travel round Britain, housesitting for friends and staying in hostels, B & Bs and cheap hotels. The home education for our children in the Lakes will consist of poetry, art and history via Wordsworth and Wainwright and of course geography as we observe hanging valleys and glaciated features.

We leave in early June. After a week north of the border in Dalmally, where we stay with Nicola's brother Drew who has gone fishing on the River Orchy, we travel south again to a rented holiday cottage for a week in Cockermouth.

Cockermouth is on the flatter ground west of Keswick, but is a good base for buses into the mountains. There's a friendly bookshop, several restaurants and a pub with its own microbrewery, the Bitter End. Our rented cottage in Bridge Street has a back yard overlooking the gently-flowing River Greta — we have no idea that two years later in 2009 the floods will cover the whole street and most of the town. Our children are fascinated by the bats that emerge from under the bridge at dusk.

Wordsworth seems to have lived just about everywhere in the Lakes. We visit his early family home in the middle of Cockermouth, now run by the National Trust, where William's father worked for Lord Lowther. The girls spend a happy morning dressing up as Dorothy and William, playing with 18th century wooden dolls and hobbyhorses, and quizzing the servants about life in 1777. They discover that the loos were often disguised as chest-of-drawers, table cutlery was laid facing downwards and that young girls wore bone bodices called stays.

Exploring the town centre we discover that by Sainsbury's there's a pleasingly eccentric statue of local hero Robinson Mitchell, who invented the auction system and set up the first auction in Cockermouth. Situated on a plinth, Mitchell only appears from the waist up, looking a little like Davros from *Doctor Who*. His left arm is in the air in auctioneer pose but has lost its hand to vandals, while his right hand has had a gavel prized away. The local paper reveals there have been a lot of problems with youths putting plastic bags over his handless arm. Clearly there's not a lot going on in Cockermouth during the long winter nights.

Nicola befriends an elderly local lady in a nearby cottage who once heard Wainwright speak in the village hall. She joins us for tea by the river when it's Lola's ninth birthday. We have Ben and Jerry's ice cream, jelly babies, cakes, tea and juice sitting at a table with a tablecloth. Earlier that day Lola and family have visited the Cumbrian Heavy Horse Centre, where she travels in a horse and cart pulled by a Fell pony called Poppy and sits on a huge Clydesdale horse called Robbie who also starred in the film, *Miss Potter*.

Our family trek up to Skiddaw, the fourth highest mountain in the Lake District, begins from Keswick. Can our young children — and indeed their parents — make it?

The weather is good, it's clear on the way up and there's just enough cloud and wind on the summit to make it feel like we really are at the top of Britain. The girls power walk up the track using a combination of isotonic Minstrels for Nell and pear drops for Lola. A number of distractions help the kids forget about the effort involved. They marvel at crazy fell-runners in trainers and shorts training for the Bob Graham Round. We chat to anyone with a dog — canines always interest our daughters. There's a woman who recently coaxed her five-year-old up Snowdon in Wales and a Dutch couple wheeling their all-terrain pram and child halfway up the mountain. Lunch is a chance to rest on my survival bag and eat tasty sandwiches.

Glimpses of Herdwick sheep help keep the kids interested too. Just as we reach the "death zone" — think Mallory in his tweeds on Everest wondering if he should carry on or go back down for a pub dinner — our group is sagging a little. It's then that the caterpillars appear.

The grass is moving. On the upper slopes of Skiddaw we find thousands of brown striped antler moth caterpillars dining out on the hillside grass. This phenomenon occurs once a decade we later learn, and it's amazing to see. They're on Helvellyn too, we're told by a fellow walker. The girls give several wriggling caterpillars a ride in their woolly hats, naming them Catriona, Katya and Cat Stevens. Caterpillars don't make great pets though, as the girls soon discover that they do lots of tiny green poos. They are rapidly liberated.

After three and a half hours Lola trots to the summit first, followed by Nell and Nicola with myself a diplomatic last. As Nell points out this is because her dad was so busy "talking to dragons", which is perhaps a first on Skiddaw. The girls feel proud and so do we as we stand by the trig point taking in the views over the sparkling ocean to the Isle of Man and inland across Derwent Water. It's a family Everest we've climbed — my children are now capable of mountain climbing and soon my daughters' young limbs will be outspeeding their parents.

Our next trip is to Carlisle for a grand power tour of the Cumbrian coast. The stations on the coastal line south from Carlisle to Barrow-in-Furness gives a glimpse of another Cumbria, more gritty and working class — Dalston, Wigton, Aspatria, Maryport, Flimby, Workington, Harrington, Parton, Whitehaven, Corkickle, St Bees, Nethertown, Braystones, Sellafield…

This side of the county is cut off from the rest of England by the considerable bulk of the Lakeland fells, but in its grand isolation has become something of a haven for wind power generation. Just north of Workington we see the outlines of white turbines dotted across the sea, as well as numerous turbines inland.

The railway is surprisingly close to the sea and Sellafield station has been blasted by salt water as shift workers wait to travel home. The phone box we use is brown and rusting as we ring to ask if the visitors' centre is open. They immediately send a minibus to pick us up from the station. Sellafield is clearly desperate for good PR and makes every effort to help us.

Alan our driver has worked at Sellafield for 21 years and happily chats about his son, also employed there. The plant still employs 9,000 local people even though it's being decommissioned and many Cumbrians are avidly pro-nuclear.

The *Doctor Who*-like visitors' centre, all silver piping and corridors, contains more friendly staff and is free to enter. The children receive free pencils, wristbands and 'bangers', pieces of card and paper that make a pleasing bang. It has interactive games (you jump on various circles to represent each power source) devised by the Science Museum and an area for the kids to make badges and draw.

The displays are surprisingly even-handed, with the argument that nuclear power is green carbon-free energy balanced by a section on the risks of nuclear terrorism; the 1986 Chernobyl accident in Russia that resulted in 28 immediate deaths and an estimated 10,000 cancers; Sellafield's (then called Windscale) own near-catastrophe that may eventually result in an extra 30 cancers in the area; and the fact that no-one knows how to dispose of nuclear waste safely for the next few thousand years. We leave with loads of free gifts, a vague idea about atoms, and a lift back to the station. It's a surprisingly enjoyable trip. Plus of course, the kids all leave with a healthy glow.

We later visit the old industrial towns of Maryport and Whitehaven, built on the declining industries of mining and sea trade. Whitehaven has some grand Georgian houses and a fine harbour. There's a maritime festival going on, where Lola dons a harness to go up a mobile climbing wall. It's all very scenic with the harbour doted with yachts, though we're surprised to see men in suits handing out leaflets for the BNP. There's a sense of working-class folk being left behind here. If Wordsworth were writing today he might forget noble shepherds and pen verse on blokes in rugby league shirts and England football kits packing out the Wetherspoon's pub.

Changing buses at Workington in the rain, we discover

that it has the first covered bus station in the UK, built in 1927. "I told you the Lakes are full of interesting facts," I say to Nicola. No doubt the roof is very useful in the downpours, but even enthusiastic travellers like us struggle to get too excited by this Workington first, though it is probably of great interest to bus station connoisseurs.

One thing that really excites the children in Carlisle is the Cursing Stone. This 14-ton polished granite rock is set in an underpass between the town and the castle.

The curse was created in 1525 by Bishop of Glasgow, Gavin Dunbar, in a bid to control the troublesome Border Reivers forever. The word "reiver" is derived from "bereaved" because that's how the Reivers, basically very violent cattle raiders, left anyone who got in their way. We read some of the splenetic curse:

"I curse them gangand (going), and I curse them rydand (riding); I curse thaim standand, and I curse thaim sittand; I curse them etand, I curse thaim drankand; I curse them walkand, I curse thaim sleepand; I curse thaim rysand, I curse thaim lyand; I curse thaim at hame, I curse thaim fra hame; I curse thaim within the house, I curse thaim without the house; I curse tahir wiffis, thair barnis, and thair servandis paticipand with thaim in thair deides..."

You get the general idea. There's more cursing than when Bill Grundy interviewed the Sex Pistols. There are 1069 words of this, so perhaps the Bishop could have done with a good copy editor.

It was installed for the Millennium celebrations by artist Andy Altman and designed by stonemason Gordon Young (born in Carlisle and with a Reiver name himself). The names of dodgy families are carved into the underpass, some in larger fonts. Here they all are: Armstrong, Graham, Noble, Robson, Watson, Young and many others. These days we'd probably deter them with some piped classical music and an asbo. It's possible the cursing stone has been too effective — some locals blamed the stone for subsequent floods, foot and mouth disease and Carlisle FC being relegated.

There's time for a solo climb as Nicola stays in town with the girls. The Honister Rambler bus drops me at Honister Pass where the slate mine has been reopened. You can go underground, put your purchase on the slate and even buy tea and pasties before ascending Dale Head.

The bus has done much of the ascent, so it's a relatively short but steep climb from the road up to Dale Head for stupendous views down the Newlands valley. Then it's a ridge walk across to the summit of Robinson and a path down steep rocks and then boggy sphagnum moss into Buttermere — which in the sun with its twin pubs and café and white cottages looks like something out of a Richard Curtis movie. All topped off by a bus back to Cockermouth and a pint of Three Hares in the Bitter End.

Our summer sojourn moves on to places like Edinburgh, Aberdeen, Wooler, Bedale, Whitley Bay, Wakefield and Eyemouth. We've got to know our country a lot better and it's all been infinitely preferable to sitting on some sweltering tourist beach.

Eventually we end up back in the Lake District wild camping for four nights in the woods by Tom's boathouse on Ullswater. He's proving a very generous host, lending us his land while he's away. We've set up a family-sized tent and listen to the sound of rain on canvas. On the fire pit we cook croissants stuffed with veggie sausages, plus waffles and chocolate bananas. Pudding is apricots stuffed with chocolate. At night we listen to the sound of noisy owls.

"Oh for goodness sake!" declares Nicola when I mutter a little about our outdoor toilet arrangements in the morning. These involve unspeakable activities with trowels and loo paper, burying the evidence among the trees, bracken, thistles, nettles and flies. Often amid a deluge. I decide that Thomas Crapper, inventor of the original water closet, was a much-neglected genius. The good thing is we've finally hired a car, so soon the girls and I became expert at restraining nature and holding on until the café at the perhaps aptly-named Pooley Bridge, which has a comparatively luxurious outside loo with cold water and a mirror.

The other alternative is the National Trust toilets at Aira Force (smelly but effective). The main waterfall plummets 65 feet and is set in a rocky gorge covered in ferns, moss and trees. From the falls we follow the path up towards Gowbarrow Fell. We decide to climb it without a packed lunch and have a picnic of Smarties at the top. We climb down as it starts to rain and when a bus finally arrives we encounter one of the region's more curmudgeonly bus drivers, who complains that our tickets are wet. This would be a little unusual in Marbella, but you'd think he might be used to the odd wet ticket in the Lakes. The driver then mistakes Nell for a boy announcing to Nicola, "tell him to sit down!" He's yet to be forgiven in our household.

Meanwhile our adventures are getting plenty of online views. Lola writes on the blog: "I don't much like going to the loo in the wood because... you can use your imagination. It makes you think what it would be like to live without a permanent roof. I miss toilets, laptops, telephones and beds. Daddy misses coffee." While Nell writes: "Mummy says that you have to have lots of treats if it's raining a lot when you camp. I miss toilets, cutlery and plates/bowls and a pillow."

Having a car means we can drive up the gear-shuddering gradients of the Kirkstone Pass and also climb up Hallin Fell, nicknamed "the motorists' fell" because it's only a few minutes walk to the top from the road and the reward is a full view of Ullswater and its mountains. We drive to Ambleside and on to Beatrix Potter's 17th century farmhouse at Hill Top in Sawrey.

With its dark wooden furnishings, dresser, rocking chair and fire you half expect Potter to pop in from a walk outside observing fungi or instructing her shepherds. The village is rammed with coach parties — her illustrations really seem to appeal to the Japanese. We imagine Potter at work here, with her desk by the window so she could get the light. We learn from a guide that the *Tale of Samuel Whiskers* contains lots of pictures of Hill Top Farm in it and Nell finds the staircase, the red curtain, the fireplace, the rolling pin and dish rack all still here.

Nicola and myself are a little jealous as we learn that Beatrix Potter was able to buy the farm from the sales of her first book, *Peter Rabbit*. The proceeds from our books so far would be lucky to buy a manhole cover in London.

We walk up to Moss Eccles Tarn, which inspired Potter's *The Tale of Mr Jeremy Fisher*. Lola and Nell pretend to be Hunca Munca and Tom Thumb (from *The Tale of Two Bad Mice*) and run all around the rocks pretending to be scampering down mouseholes.

When there's a rare fine day on Ullswater Nicola drives me to Pooley Bridge and the start of the walk up to the High Street range. What have the Romans ever done for us? Well, as fans of *Life of Brian* will know, they did manage to build the original High Street at a height of more than 700 metres (or 2,500 feet), stretching for 18 miles across the Lake District.

Walking up from Pooley Bridge it's fascinating to reflect that I'm following the path of Roman Legions who used to trek between forts at Ambleside and Penrith, covering 20 miles every five hours across the mountains, before relaxing in a hot bath full of Roman Radox.

First there's an intriguing detour to the Cockpit, a Neolithic standing stone circle — or did the Romans put them there just to keep *Time Team* busy? Then a yomp across boggy grass and moss up to the mountain plateau. As my boots become saturated, even in July, I reflect just how hard it must have been for Italian geezers in sandals longing for olive oil and sundried tomatoes. You can still see where the Romans used the gradient of the rock to facilitate their progress. As my boots sink in the peaty mulch once more, the attraction of a decent surface and camber becomes obvious.

Also in evidence is the Romans' unsentimental approach to walking. The path skirts all the stunning views over Ullswater and sticks resolutely to the drab upland commons – although the views are much more spectacular near the High Street summit. It was a military road all about safe passage and concealment from hostile Scots, Cumbrians and Geordies. No time for Wainwright guidebooks here.

After two and a half hours I make it across eroded peat and water pools to the summit of Loadpot Hill. It's really just a hill in the middle of a wide grassy plateau, but the views across to the Helvellyn range are good.

The path continues for another four miles to the summit of High Street where the locals held horse races 200 years ago. But for me it's time to return for a pint at Pooley Bridge. Maybe it's best the Romans left these shores some 1,600 years ago. If they were still in control the M6 would probably head straight across Lakeland's most loved peaks.

Meanwhile the water level continues to rise on Ullswater. The lake edges closer to our tent each night as the rains continue. The papers are full of pictures of places like Tewkesbury underwater as floods hit the West Country, Yorkshire and much of northern England. We wonder if it's due to climate change and if our attempt to claim the moral high ground by staying in Britain will result in our tent being swept away.

Before the waters rise again, we move on to the north-east, where I discover that camping has taken its toll on an unreconstructed Londoner. A large red blotch appears on my foot while we're in Greenlaw on the Scottish borders and the doctor says it's a combination of cellulitis, athlete's foot and a sprained ankle, bought on by too much boot wearing during our trip. Not exactly a Sir Ranulph Fiennes-style injury. Some antibiotics soon cure my plates of meat, as we say in Essex.

That year is bookended by the death of both of my parents. In the autumn my sister and I have lunch with my dad in Norfolk. That evening, after we return home, my dad has a stroke and dies in hospital the next night. We'd clashed over many things, not least my refusal to become a farmer. He was a man of his time and his attitudes to socialists, foreigners, women and gay people all seemed, to me, dated and rooted in Empire. Yet somewhere he had the same urges as me; he'd walked the Pennine Way in his late fifties and loved to tour the Scottish Highlands and Ireland. He had climbed Ben Nevis and Snowdon. It was my dad who passed on my first pair of walking boots and a survival bag. Now a long year of acting as executor of my dad's estate and the sad task of clearing out my parents' home has to begin.

Although it has been an epic summer away and we've seen some fabulous places. We've started to walk Hadrian's Wall, seen seals feeding in the harbour at Eyemouth, climbed Ben Lomond, drunk tea in the Rondezvous Café at Whitley Bay, walked dogs on the vast clear beaches of Lindisfarne, seen rock climbers at Malham Cove, released a bird trapped in a lobster pot in Pennan, been attacked by midges in Dalmally, swum in the country's only heated seawater outdoor pool at Stonehaven and visited the poison garden at Alnwick Castle.

But is there anywhere more attractive than the Lake District? Somehow it seems to be just the right mix of rugged and accessible, mountains that are vast without being quite as intimidating as the Scottish Munros, with houses made of local stone blending with hill and rock, dry stone walls merging into the landscape, streams meandering and clear water gushing over boulders in deserted valleys. Plus inviting pubs at the end of every trek and the human stories of local characters like Potter, Ruskin, Wordsworth and Wainwright. For all our travels, it's still my favourite part of Britain.

8. ANOTHER STONE IN THE WALL

Spring 2008

The Southern Fells

Finally my love of the Lake District is coming in useful professionally. The *Guardian's* Family Challenge column agrees to my idea of writing a piece about stone walling with my family. It's a good time to be pitching ideas. The Lakes are big on TV again, with Julia Bradbury bringing a more female-friendly feel (and better anoraks than AW) to her BBC series *Wainwright Walks*.

I've always had a thing about dry stone walls. Read Wainwright's guides and you'll find many eulogies to the unknown craftsmen who erected them over the centuries. But without mortar, how do they stay up? Trawling the internet and discovering a weekend dry stone walling course, it seems like a great excuse for a weekend in the Lakes. Only will my family share my love of northern rock?

We find ourselves among a dozen people standing in front of a dry stone wall, beneath the exquisite backdrop of the screes and peaks of the Langdale Pikes.

Our instructor is Andrew Loudon, a one-time carpenter from Manchester who is now an expert stonewaller. He's built walls everywhere from the Lakes to Hampstead, London and the USA, won several walling competitions and built stone features for the Chelsea

Flower Show.

Andrew's health and safety talk is suitably gritty. "These stones can bite," he warns, before giving us a choice of gloves or no gloves. Andrew prefers to get his hands dirty, and I opt to do the same, wanting to feel at one with the ancient volcanic rocks.

Then we divide into two teams, one either side of the wall, and start to dismantle a five-metre section of wall, suffering from bulges. We lay the top stones a few metres from the wall and then start to remove the face stones. Between the two sets of face stones is the packing, a jumble of small filler rocks. They are completely dry and give off the whiff of cordite, caused by a chemical reaction from the stones touching each other.

Some of the walls in Cumbria were built in the 12th century, the higher ones on the fells as late as the Napoleonic Wars. Has Andrew ever found any artefacts inside the walls? "The best thing I ever found was a crisp packet with a competition for the Olympics on the back! I did once find a knuckle joint in the wall every seven metres — it was where the waller had stopped to have his lunch each day!"

The kids enjoy stacking the packing stones in a pile as we dismantle the wall level by level, the bigger stones coming from the foundations. They enjoy finding a shocked toad inside the packing at ground level. After a couple of hours we have a dismantled wall on the grass and little idea how to reassemble it. The children have lost interest in the dismantling, instead going to a separate pile of stones and creating their own circular enclosure. "It's a shelter for the lambs," explains Nell.

After lunch we get to work rebuilding the wall from the jumbled pile of stones at our feet. Andrew has stuck reinforcing bars into the ground at either end of the existing wall and tied a piece of string between them so we can build straight — "Your wall should be twice as wide at the bottom as at the top."

We try to make our wall's face stay level with the straight line of the string, starting with the larger stones as foundations. Andrew is a laid-back instructor, inspecting the stones with the eye of a craftsman and offering occasional suggestions such as "You just need a bit more packing there Pete to level that off... turn that big one round there so the strength goes in to the wall."

"They should do this on *The Apprentice*," suggests Nicola.

Tom, a 15-year-old doing the course as an extension of his Geography studies is a conscientious worker, but our own children soon give up lugging large stones. Instead they relish the freedom of charging around the green fields behind us. Bizarrely, we've discovered that Ruth, a stonewaller helping Andrew with the course, knows Nicola from their time working together in the Solomon Islands. Our girls team up with her daughter Megan and start to paddle barefoot up a small stream. "We've been put in prison for something we didn't do and now we're escaping," explains Lola. Then they explore the upper fields and return with the gory news: "Guess how many dead lambs we saw, six with their heads bitten off and one we saw alive earlier!"

Meanwhile our wall is making real progress. Andrew moves the string up with each level. It's satisfying work. Mark, an IT expert doing the course, says he enjoys it because if there's a mistake here it's his fault and not the computer's. The secret seems to be in placing your packing carefully rather than throwing it in and getting a flat top to each level.

By the end of the afternoon we're placing the top stones on our new wall. My hands are scuffed, scoured and dirty but there's a real sense of achievement in our group. But not among Nell, who complains loudly that the wallers have dismantled her lamb shelter to add to the packing. We promise her a new shelter tomorrow. Our wall even looks quite straight and tapers at the top. "Not bad," says Andrew. We celebrate in the Old Dungeon Ghyll Hotel with a pint and for the kids, crisps. Then we bus it back to our family room at the Gables guest house in Ambleside.

The next day we return to our wall in Langdale to break down and reassemble another section. The morning rain results in numerous worms emerging to amuse the girls.

"Andrew says the last time someone touched these rocks was 300 years ago," I tell my daughters.

"Cool!" says Lola,

They soon tire of dismantling the wall though, and so, with permission, set off to scale Side Pike, with instructions to keep us in sight. An hour later they return, exhilarated at having the independence to scale a 1000-foot hill — "Daddy, we climbed a mountain!"

This wall's foundations are huge boulders that require a pick-axe, crow-bar and much lifting to remove. But our wall eventually comes down and this time we reassemble it with fancy cross pieces (long flat pieces of stone) placed across the upper parts of the wall to provide greater durability.

To enthuse our children Andrew suggests we place a time capsule inside the wall. It works brilliantly. Lola writes "My name is Lola and I know about climate change" followed by the date and names of all us stonewallers. Nell draws a picture of herself building the wall and writes, "My name is Nell and I am the best artist". They place both notes inside a plastic water bottle and place it in the wall for some future *Time Team*-types to discover. The kids then disappear to the nearby farm where they spend two hours cooing over hand-reared lambs.

Soon we've rebuilt the wall again. A car of tourists stops to take our picture. "There's nowt to it really, it's just stacking stones," says Andrew, though really he's a lot more skilful than that. For us it feels like we've created a sculpture worthy of Andy Goldsworthy.

On the bus back to Ambleside we're still discussing our stone love. "I liked the way you put the baby rocks in the middle," says Lola. "It was a little bit interesting," says a tactful Nell. Meanwhile Nicola is gazing out of the window with a poetic air.

"That's a lovely top," she sighs.

"Yes, I've always loved the Langdale Pikes."

"No, not the Pikes, the wall we're driving past!"

Once we travelled to the Lake District to look at mountains. Now, all in all, we just want to place another stone in the wall.

Nicola takes the children back to London for school while I'm allowed an extra day in Ambleside. This gives me a chance to return to Dungeon Ghyll and complete Wainwright's circular route up to Crinkle Crags, named because their crinkled outlines are recognisable from miles around.

It's a splendid route walking up Oxendale and then past the ravine of Browney Gill, where stunted trees cling at extreme angles to the damp rocks and white waterfalls plummet all the way up to Red Tarn. The path turns right, upwards across peaty grassland before the crinkles emerge. There are three main peaks plus another two smaller crinkles.

As Wainwright says, it's one of the best ridge walks in Lakeland. Each crinkle is a serrated dome of shattered rock, offering a pulpit to sit in and admire the views dropping down to Oxendale and across to the Langdale Pikes. There is a saddle between each crag and some rewarding scrambling to negotiate my way round the Bad Step. It's down to the Three Tarns walkers' crossroad for stunning views of the crumpled-pastry rockface of the links of Bowfell, sitting atop a mass of scree. From here it's downhill along the Band and back to Dungeon Ghyll.

While every wall I walk past on the way up and down, some now sadly tumbling into the grass, brings a new sense of admiration for the men and women who built them, section by section, with scuffed hands and aching arms, all those years ago.

9. THE BEST INN IN THE WORLD

Summer 2009 — Summer 2012

The Western Fells, the Southern Fells

W e've finally made it to the Wasdale Head Inn. It's been a dream to stay there since glimpsing Wastwater from the top of Great Gable. The hotel and pub is in the most remote section of the Lakes, but our family make the whole journey without a car in the summer of 2009. When we phoned the Wasdale Head Inn to book our rooms, the staff had helpfully suggested an adventurous route for non-drivers, which involved three train journeys and a yomp over the fells from Boot.

We travel north from London and after an overnight stay in Carlisle, we take the rambling coast line to Ravenglass, as young Nell amuses herself by playing hoola-hoop in the luggage compartment. From Ravenglass we take what appears to be a Noddy train, but is in fact the Ravenglass and Eskdale Railway. This narrow gauge railway was originally built in 1873 to take iron ore from Boot to Ravenglass. In 1876 it became the first narrow gauge railway in Britain open to passengers. When granite mining operations ceased the railway was saved by the Wakefield family at the start of the 1960s and re-opened as a tourist attraction.

After a cup of tea and tasty cakes at Jan's station café we join the many tourists and board an open carriage that can barely contain our suitcases. There's a gush of steam and a tiny engine starts to chug towards the fells, accompanied by several toots on the train's horn. For Lola, now 11 and Nell, 8, there's a delightful Harry Potter-esque quality to our journey. We travel through woods, with Nicola encouraging the girls to look out for red squirrels, Herdwick sheep, ash, rowan and elder trees and curlews flying above us.

The slower we travel the more we seem to enjoy it. Eventually our tiny train deposits us at Dalegarth station, at the foot of the fells. We then hand our luggage over to a mate of the hotel owner who is going to drive our cases over to the Wasdale Head Inn. There's no charge for this and the staff at the Inn seem genuinely keen to help us make the journey without hiring a car.

We walk into Boot and discover two idyllic looking pubs, before having a quick picnic and exploring Lakeland's oldest working water mill, standing by a packhorse bridge over Whillan Beck. The admission signs offers discounts for "recycled kids" and "dustbin lids", adding, "experts not admitted". We watch the gentle rotation of the water wheel and see flour being ground. The first official record of the Eskdale Mill comes in 1294, but it's built to a Roman design and it's thought milling here might go back 3000 years to the first cereal crops. It's an unexpected bonus on our journey.

From the mill we head on to the corpse road, so-named because it was the route for the dead to be taken for burial. As we emerge on to Eskdale Moor we pass a stone circle adding to the sense of antiquity. We emerge on to a bleak brown-grassed moorland with mountains all around. The path takes us towards Burnmoor Tarn, a large expanse of water without islands. We're astonished to see a pebbledashed house by the tarn. Its windows are boarded-up against the wind and rain. This is Burnmoor Lodge, originally a 19th century hunting lodge. It's now used by members of the Burnmoor Lodge Club, whose rules include the rather noble ambition, "to encourage appreciation of wild, remote and beautiful places... to allow people to improve their mental, spiritual and physical health by escaping for a while from the noise and busyness of their everyday lives."

A drizzle starts and we don our waterproofs. Nell is slithering in her Wellies because her feet have grown. "Dad, when are we ever going to get there, we've walked forever," complains Lola.

"It's that white building down there in the valley."

"But that's miles away..."

"It's going to be great when we get there, it will have pub dinners. And look at Wastwater, isn't it beautiful? And that's Great Gable and Kirk Fell ahead us."

"But it's raining."

"You'll have a real sense of achievement having walked five miles from Boot," I suggest, doubting somehow if this will be accepted.

Slowly Wasdale Head comes into focus. Big black letters spell out "INN' on the side of the whitewashed building. They are pulling me closer as I dream of beer. We arrive by the headland of Wastwater viewing the massive banks of scree cascading towards the shoreline. We cross a footbridge and we're back on a flat path across dayglow green fields. And finally we're at the reception of the Wasdale Head Inn. It's old and beamed and has that lovely feeling of not having changed for decades. A small shop called the Barn Door offers a mix of hiking equipment and baked beans for the campers in the field opposite.

Taking the keys to our self-contained apartment of Beck Head we enter and all thoughts of juvenile mutiny are forgotten. It has two bedrooms, a living room with a video player, books and board games. There's a kitchen for self-catering and in our room the skylight has a brilliant view of the slopes of Kirk Fell, with a path heading directly to the top. No chance of route problems there.

We head to the bar for a pub dinner. The residents' bar is a wonderful sanctuary, covered in wood panels and full of climbing memorabilia, with old boots, ice picks, weather reports and photos of men in tweed climbing Napes Needle on Great Gable. For the Wasdale Head Inn is the home of British rock climbing. It was from here that Walter Parry Haskett Smith, an old Etonian and Oxford man, first climbed Napes Needle in 1886 with just heavy boots and an old school tie. Owen Glynne Jones followed, a London-born climber famed for his gymnastic stunts around the Wasdale Head Inn bar, presumably after a sherbet or two.

The public bar at Wasdale is called Ritson's Bar, named after Will Ritson a former landlord of the Inn and the self-proclaimed 'World's Biggest Liar'. More recently Mr Wainwright would have sat in this very bar too, bemoaning the red and orange blobs on the fellsides. It oozes atmosphere, Lakeland kudos and beer.

There's a micro-brewery here and an array of fine ales named after mountains. The dark Yewbarrow ale becomes a favourite of mine, though customers can choose from many ales with names like Great Gable and Lingmell.

We eat a hearty dinner in the bar and retreat to sit on the wooden terrace outside our apartment. We take in the stunning view of fields and a patchwork of dry stone walls seguing into the grand crags of Great Gable, Scafell Pike and Lingmell.

The next day we explore the smallest church in Lakeland. The Church of St Olaf (it was nameless until 1977) is a simple but splendid single storey building hunched into the ground hunkering against the wind. It can be dated until at least 1550 but the beams are said to come from a Viking longship. St Olaf's has long been associated with climbers and there's a moving monument to local climbers who died in the first world war.

We walk along Moses' Trod to the walkers' crossroads of Sty Head. Our daughters seem keen now, and enjoy throwing rocks into the tarn. We realize Great Gable is only 300 metres climb away and make a determined effort to head left up to the summit. We climb a staircase of loose stones and it turns misty. Nell is enchanted by being inside cloud. "Are we really in the clouds? It's like flying!" We make the top and it's the second big mountain the kids have made it up.

The real reason we are here is as a treat for my 50th birthday. Was it really 34 years ago that I was scaling Langdale Pikes in DMs on my geography field trip? My birthday begins with opening cards and some presents from Nicola, which change my life: a pair of Lexi waking poles from the Barn Door shop and a

Wainwright wallchart. This splendid invention includes a summit tick and date list and a 3-D relief map of the Lake District.

The peaks are listed in order from number one, Scafell Pike at 3210 feet to number 214, Castle Crag at 985 feet (300 metres), the only Wainwright peak below 1000 feet. My pen finger starts to itch with a desire to tick the boxes and add the notes of the date each peak was scaled. Nicola also buys me a map of "tubular fells", which has the names of all the fells placed on a London Underground-style map (this is later framed and placed on our landing).

While Nicola takes the girls around Wastwater, I have the chance to go on a solo circular walk of the Mosedale Horseshoe as a birthday treat. The rear of the Inn faces out to Mosedale, an uninhabited valley with just a beck and a wall of mountains at its head. It's a sublime spot. Using a photocopy of Wainwright's circular walk, I follow his directions up to Pillar on the right hand side of the ridge. The more you walk the more the Lake District starts to fit together. From the ridge I can gaze down into the wooded depths of Ennerdale, with the High Stile range the other side of the valley, still familiar from our Coast to Coast walk. Now it's a relatively easy horseshoe walk from summit to summit but with a dip into the evocatively named Wind Gap and then I'm peering down Mirk Cove, an equally splendidly-named drop into a stony abyss.

From Scoat Fell I take Wainwright's recommended diversion to Steeple, so named because the summit is just a few yards wide and offers a visionary view out to the Irish Sea. It seems a good place to contemplate 50 years of life. Milestones have been passed: marriage, mortgage, books, and children. I'm lucky. My kids are healthy and adorable, my wife buys me wall-charts and I'm still fit enough to do this.

The day's final summit is Red Pike, making it five Wainwrights that can be ticked off on my new wall chart, not that I'm counting. Descent is not easy though. It's a very steep scree chute where I find myself running from rock to rock causing minor avalanches, desperately seeking the grassy edges and then cascading bottom first for some the way, ending up with red soil-encrusted trousers and battered ankles. Quite a few expletives echo around the empty valley.

But once down it's a happy walk along the valley to the glorious packhorse bridge at Wasdale Head and then into our apartment. We all celebrate with chocolate cake and pasta and then take some drinks from the bar back to our room. Lola and Nell perform a special play, which involves them dressing up in over-sized waterproofs, carrying a map case and pretending to be mum and dad. Their routine seems to involve a lot of arguing over routes and snacks, so it's clearly a project based solely on their imaginations. It's been a memorable birthday.

Our stay at Wasdale is a short one for we depart to finish the Hadrian's Wall path, completing the final leg from Carlisle to Bowness-in-Solway. We end the trail sitting in a Roman-esque recreation of an Edwardian viewing point, looking across the sweeping expanse of the Solway Firth towards the hills of Scotland. But we vow to return to Wasdale and spend other summers there.

The following year we're back. On my 51st birthday I

climb Scafell by the steep scramble of Lord's Rake and the west level traverse, an exciting rocky scramble. Some fellow walkers even look quite impressed when I emerge from out of a rocky cleft on to the summit. I find Scafell more satisfying than its slightly higher but over-populated neighbour of Scafell Pike.

We all scale Scafell Pike the following day, fortified by Haribos, and the girls are delighted to discover that there is mobile phone reception on top. My mobile tells me that West Ham have lost 3-0 on the opening game of the season, so perhaps enforced silence was preferable. On the way back to the Inn there's a mini mutiny as the girls object to talk of home-cooked cheap pasta and chant "we want a pub dinner!" all the way back. We relent and buy them one.

It's interesting to be sitting on top of Scafell Pike having just read Wordsworth's *Guide to the Lakes*. The great poet wrote his guide in 1810 as a hack job to pay the bills, but it's fascinating to read today. The journey that is completed by thousands every summer now was quite an adventure back then.

Describing a walk up what he calls "Scaw-fell Pike", the great man of the Lakes has to employ a local guide, a "wise man of the mountains" to take his party to the top one October. When they reach the top after much toil, it is surprisingly wind-free. Wordsworth describes his "repast", including eating provisions out of brown paper, and bemoans the fact that there is no water (unlike on Great Gable where a hollow always contains water) to "temper our beverage". The poet mistakes a cloud for a ship on the sea, only to be corrected by his guide. He sees no sign of the impending storm, but the guide, with the expert eye of the shepherd, has seen it coming from near Whitehaven. For all his wanderings around lakes and daffodils, Wordsworth seems, reassuringly to me, a bit of an amateur when it comes to bagging summits.

On another day our walk to Illgill Head, the peak above the astonishing Wastwater screes, sees us discussing the grim subject of bodies in the lake. In 1984 a diver searching for a missing French student found Margaret Hogg's body 110 feet down in Wastwater, wrapped in carpet and still well-preserved due to the lack of oxygen in the water. Peter Hogg had strangled his wife after a row in 1976, and then travelled up from Surrey to row out into the lake and dump the body. Hogg went to prison for manslaughter and the case soon became known in the press as "the lady in the lake" case. It's a tragic and sordid story to associate with "Britain's favourite view".

We drive in a hired car to a hound show at Rydal, travelling over Wrynose Pass. Nicola is the more experienced driver and handles the gear-crunching and passing points with aplomb as we pass peaks with evocative names like Cold Pike. At the hound show we meet our old friends Fleur and Richard, tweedy Yorkshire folk who seem entirely at home among the men in brown coats and red-faced farming folk in the beer tent.

We drive down to the Wastwater screes and the girls play on a tiny island, enjoying the frisson of jumping over two feet of water and being queens of their own tiny land, with the majestic scree behind them. It makes a great picture and remains a lasting image of their childhood.

We return in other summers, though we haven't given up on international travel entirely. After ten years of non-flying we take a three-month family trip to Australia and the Solomon Islands in 2011. The Solomon Islands is full of friendly people, beautiful lagoons and beaches, but also lots of not particularly friendly wildlife. On Tetepare Island our guides bark like dogs and call over crocodiles from the other side of the lake. Sharks swim in the bay. We encounter monitor lizards, snakes, a nearly-decapitated possum dropped by a sea eagle, a plague of moths and myriad mosquitoes. Most dangerous is a cat that scratches Nicola's leg on Lola Island, causing it to go septic within hours in the tropical heat.

At our friend's house in Honiara we discover that the strange noises under a bed have been coming from an escaped coconut crab intended for the cooking pot, its giant pincers ready to crush the most vulnerable parts of my body. Exploring the south sea tropics is a great experience, but perhaps searching for red squirrels is a little more sedate.

The next year we return to Wasdale and I get to climb Yewbarrow, proving to myself that it's more than just the name of a pint of great beer. It might only be 2000 feet high but it's a tough scramble up to the top and it's surprisingly challenging. On the top I discover on my Nokia mobile that West Ham have beaten Aston Villa 1-0. Strange how some mountains become indelibly associated with football results.

Getting back from a walk is always a pleasure. It's difficult to get to, but at the Wasdale Head Inn you feel enclosed in an amphitheatre of glorious mountains and uninhabited valleys. It's just you, the sheep and a select group of hardy National Trust farmers. The world can't touch you at Wasdale and no mobile phone signal can penetrate the monoliths around. When the sun sets over the mountains and all is bathed in yellow light at the end of the day it's a place of utter tranquility. In the bar dark wood is reflected in the pints of bitter, chips cool, cheese oozes over lasagna, apartment duvets await tired limbs and all is well in the Lakes.

10. HIGH STILE COUNSELLOR

Autumn 2009

The Western Fells

Guides to the Lake District are not a new innovation. William Wordsworth had a go at one with his *Guide to the Lakes* published in 1810. There's a fine tale of an unworldly clergyman who asked him if he had written anything else. Wordsworth's work followed William Gilpin's pithily-titled 1778 tome, *Observations, relative chiefly to picturesque beauty, made in the year 1772, on several parts of England; particularly the mountains, and lakes of Cumberland, and Westmoreland.*

In the twentieth century Wainwright produced his *Pictorial Guide to the Lakeland Fells* in seven books from 1954 to 1965. Later writers devoted books to touring the Lakes. Hunter Davies wrote his excellent *A Walk Around The Lakes* in 2000 and also helped reveal the real man behind the line drawings in *Wainwright: The Biography*. Specialist publishers such as Lonely Planet and the Rough Guide have both launched updated guides to the Lake District for travellers and backpackers.

But one of the first authors of a Lakeland guide is relatively unknown today. Thomas West wrote his *Guide to the Lakes of Cumberland, Westmorland and Lancashire* in 1778. It was one of the first guidebooks to the region and thanks to Amazon a copy is now in my hands. What's striking is how terrifying Mr West found mountains. On his horse and carriage journey from Keswick to Buttermere he frets about, "rude and awful mountains that tower to the skies in a variety of grotesque forms, and on their murky furrowed sides hang many a torrent."

At Buttermere he fearfully views the High Stile range, providing, "the highest possible contrast in nature. Four spiral towering mountains, dark, dun and gloomy at noon-day, rise immediately from the western extremity of the deep narrow dell and hang over Buttermere."

Writers like West couldn't quite escape the previous notions of the gentry that mountains were useless, unpleasant and a bit scary. Daniel Defoe, being a Stoke Newington lad, was quite lost in the Lakes a century earlier. He described them in 1698 as the "wildest, the most barren and frightful" place he had ever seen.

Thomas West was born in Scotland in 1720 but was educated abroad. We know that he was ordained as a Catholic priest and studied natural philosophy on the continent, but returned to live at Furness, aged 54, in 1774. Semi-retired in the Lakes he had already penned an earlier book *The Antiquities of Furness*. He developed a sideline in taking the gentry on tours of the Lakes and pitched his book at, "persons of genius, taste and observation." The guide proved a nice little earner and went on to a further eight editions after West's death in 1779.

The route on to the three-for-two tables lay in making a bid for the picturesque market. In the 18th century there was a vogue for educating the *nouveau riche* in matters of aesthetics. Among other writers, Edmund Burke published, *A Philosophical Enquiry into the Origin of our Ideas of the Sublime and the Beautiful.*" In 1768 William Gilpin published *An Essay on Prints,* in which he came up with the theory of the Picturesque, an aesthetic ideal somewhere between the Beautiful and the Sublime.

In keeping with this picturesque ideal West advocated stopping at viewing stations. In lieu of a digital camera, West expected those following his guidebook to sit down at these viewing stations and knock out a watercolour of a picturesque view. The person of refinement would get out something called a Claude Glass. This was a small portable mirror, with its surface tinted a dark colour to soften the view. The Claude Glass had a carrying-case and the image in the mirror was thought to give painterly tones.

Bizarrely the painter had to turn their back on the sublime views and view them in their mirror, a tactic ridiculed by 18th Century satirists. West explains it all in terms more reminiscent of an iPhone manual: "The person using it ought always to turn his back to the object that he views. It [the Claude Glass] should be suspended by the upper part of the case... holding it a little to the right or the left (as the position of the parts to be viewed require) and the face screened from the sun."

Though in practice it might not have been as aesthetic as West hoped. When West wrote his *Guide to the Lakes* most of the grand tourists were rich aristocratic young men on a kind of gap year for toffs, where they assimilated the culture of Paris, the Alps and Rome. Their accompanying tutors were known as "bearleaders" as they attempted to steer their charges from gambling away their estates or catching the clap.

I'm thinking of West as I board the bus to Buttermere outside Booth's supermarket in Keswick. West was prescient when he wrote of the need for a local guide — although at Derwent Water he recommends sending your guide away so that the traveller can experience the "sport of fancy and exercise of taste" in solitude.

Could I rank as one of West's "persons of genius, taste and observation"? It seems my guide to Buttermere in the autumn of 2009 is the driver of the Honister Rambler bus.

"Are you the bus driver?" asks a pensioner on a grand tour of Lakeland, courtesy of a free bus pass.

"No, I were going to wait till you were not looking and sneak off!" quips the bus driver, who sounds very northern and looks a bit like former *Doctor Who* star Christopher Eccleston.

The passengers pay fares or flash passes and the small single-decker bus glides into gear and out of Keswick. Soon we're heading past the shore of Derwent Water on a wooded road overhung by precipitous but inspiring rockfaces.

Our driver is speaking aloud to his passengers, giving voice to the complex interior dialogue of the bus driver's lament.

"I've done this route 73 times, so I've only got to drive this route another 27 times before the season ends. I tried to knock 'em back this morning, but our secretary's useless!" he confides. "I was down for one week on and that was two months ago!"

Like some of West's more earthy local guides, he's unmoved by the Alpine grandeur around him.

PETE MAY

"But it's the most beautiful route in the country," says a passenger.

"Oh, aye. Will I be coming back next year? Don't take this the wrong way, but no!"

An Australian passenger asks him about the problems of the route. "Oh, you get double money. But there's the problem of 40 passengers at Buttermere getting on – it means one of 'em's walking."

He looks at his blue work shirt and comments: "I wish my wife had ironed my shirt better. I'll tell her to work for a living." London ears get a little nervous at this unreconstructed banter.

"You could do it yourself! Be careful what you say to her!" says the formidable Lancastrian lady in front of me.

The driver makes a clever manoeuvre between a parked car, a van and dry stone wall. "Sometimes it hurts being so good!" he declares.

There's some dithering as a mother and daughter board. "Don't give her an option – she'll take an hour. It's like my eight year-old daughter!" A tired hiker flags the bus down. "You're lucky, I'm going that way," he tells the walker wanting Portinscale.

Then the High Stile range comes into view towards Buttermere. The bus stop is right next to a farm café selling home-made ice creams and tea and Twix, there's a tinkling stream and two homely looking pubs in the Fish Hotel and the Bridge Hotel. Slightly up a hill there's the small, single-storey chapel where Thomas West reflected that "the stipend is not large", perhaps dismissing it from his career plans.

In some ways it's still easy to understand West's

trepidation about fearsome fells. Buttermere is utterly dominated by the mass of the High Stile Range consisting of the three peaks of Red Pike, High Stile and High Crag. It feels more enclosed than the other Lakeland valleys and the fact that the Honister Rambler doesn't run after the end of October adds to the sense of isolation in winter. The village itself feels impermanent, built on a thin strip of soil between the lakes of Buttermere and Crummock Water. It's a tiny encampment of white buildings nestling beneath the High Stile range on one side and Robinson and Dale Head on the other.

There's a huge grey gash down the foot of the range, which at first I think might be a heavily eroded footpath up to Red Pike. But close-up you can see it's simply the path of Sour Milk Gill, described by West as a "roaring cataract", which has washed away all traces of topsoil leaving raw rocks and boulders.

It's three o'clock in the afternoon and the sky is clear. The Londoner in the Lakes soon learns to grab any chance of mist-free tops. I walk a few hundred yards to the youth hostel. Like most hostels it's a former grand house now full of walking boots and Twix bars on sale behind the locked reception. Its balcony has an uplifting view across the valley to the crags and would make a fine viewing station for West. If a traveller needs refreshment along with a quick glance in their Claude Glass there's a Coca-Cola vending machine on the veranda.

Reception is closed until five, so I leave my books and toilet bag in a cubbyhole in the kitchen and take the rest of my backpack with me up to Red Pike. It should just be possible to ascend directly from the village on the tourist path and be down before dark.

Red Pike is noted by West for its "ferruginous colour", suggesting a Will Self-like capacity for never using a simple word when a Radio 4-style one will do. A path from the Fish Inn crosses the grassy plain and ascends up through a small wood before taking a series of zigzags up the side of Red Pike. You can imagine West exclaiming: "Sir, have you taken leave of all rational thought ascending such a ferruginous and grotesque apparition of most monstrous form? Pray, let us retreat to the shore of Crummock Water with the Claude Glass."

West would surely approve of the upgraded path though. He complains all the way to Buttermere about the state of the roads, which he blamed on the "inattention of the dalesmen who habituate themselves to tread in the track made by their flock and wish for nothing better." Now the tourist path has been recently repaired with neatly laid stones, although it's hard upon the feet because they are not laid in steps, but form one continual toe-numbing uneven ramp.

The path levels out eventually and heads towards the rock-strewn gulf of Sour Milk Gill. The view suddenly expands into the amphitheatre above Bleaberry Tarn. The green flank of a splendid hanging valley stands above the tarn. Above that lies the ridge and descending gullies of Eagle Crag, linking Red Pike and High Stile.

West used a bit of authorial imagination in his guide, clearly having never studied glaciation in A level geography, writing of conical mountains, craters, extinct volcanoes and roaring cataracts here.

To the right of the still and reflective tarn (nature's Claude Glass?) is a red scar of a path blazed towards the summit. It climbs steeply over loose red scree, through crumbling chimneys of rock and eventually to the summit.

After my trek to the top the views stretch across Crummock Water and Buttermere and across to the screes of Whiteside Pike, the Newlands Valley and way beyond. A short stroll reveals the wooded valley of Ennerdale on the other side of the ridge far below. The Irish Sea is bathed in dimming orange sunlight and even Sellafield looks peaceful and a little sublime from up here.

As the light fades I allow an hour to descend the path again and stumble through the darkening forest to the shore of Buttermere. The perfect ascending ridge of Fleetwith Pike, sitting like a crouching dog at the far end of the lake, makes a great doorstop for the valley, as ominous darker clouds gather in the dusk.

The Fish pub is the sensible place to stop for a pint of Jennings and a mushroom stroganoff as I feel my new North Face t-shirt clinging sweatily to my back. Perhaps it's full of gentlemen and ladies in search of the picturesque.

"It was like a convention..." the grey-aged woman in a Berghaus fleece at the table behind me is telling her group, "with all these clones and dozens of Darth Vaders. But there were no Chewbaccas..."

"I'm off to the cottage to drink Newcastle Brown!" says a cheery holidaymaker, jogging out of the bar. Another table discuss Jamie Oliver restaurants, while a group of young British Asians receive vegetarian food and fair trade tea from the waitress.

"You shouldn't have to warm up your croissant. I know it's not a first class hotel…" laments an elderly chap at the bar.

Outside it's absolutely black, but thankfully my Maglite torch lights the way for my tired body to trek back to the youth hostel, noting that here you can see the stars. I'm delighted to find that modernised youth hostels now have luxuries like lamps on the top bunks. I climb the ladder and in my bunk peruse the annual report of the Cockermouth mountain rescue team that was on sale at reception.

It's grim reading — no doubt West would have loved it. Two deaths including a climber hit by a falling rock, a lightning strike on Grisedale Pike, broken wrists and ankles, dislocated knees, appalling weather conditions and hypothermic runners during a mountain marathon, and a sheep stuck on High Crag. Perhaps West was right. We get cosy in our Gore-Tex and all-year round walking world, but the mountains should be treated with respect. Rivers turn into deluges, fell runners get airlifted in atrocious conditions, rocks fall and shatter heads.

The next morning the Mountain Weather Information Service print-out at reception claims there's a 70 per cent chance of visibility on the summits. It's time to tackle all three peaks of High Stile range, armed with a photocopy of the route from *Fellwalking with Wainwright.*

Taking the path from Buttermere by the lakeside, I follow Wainwright's recommended route, a climb to Burtness Comb. There's not a single person on this path and soon I'm wandering among boulders and scree in another hanging valley, gazing up at the shattered rockface of High Crag's Sheepbone Buttress. There's no sign of Wainwright's suggested Sheepbone Rake, unless it's an ascent through what looks like a high-altitude scree slope. His path is not even on the OS map.

Chastened, I re-plan my route and follow the faint path round the bottom of the mountain and eventually join up with the lakeside path to Scarth Gap. Here two volunteers are laying stones on a well-kept path with great views of Fleetwith Pike, the valley-end of Wanscale Bottom and Haystacks.

Before Scarth Gap the path turns by a crumbling dry stone wall. It's a slog and towards the top there's half a mile of relentless thigh-burning knee-hoisting clambering over loose grey rocks.

But eventually I stumble towards the summit of High Crag, its cairn covered in a spiky sculpture of rusted fence posts. The Lakeland vista opens up before me, and the hard work of the day is over. I sit down in the shelter of some rocks and get my mobile out to send Nicola a text. "On top of High Pike! Px."

What would West make of mobiles? From his love of the Claude Glass I don't think he'd mind the odd bit of technology on the fells. In fact he'd probably include a couple of paragraphs on how to use a mobile with refinement and taste and not immediately see if you've got reception once you're on top of a summit.

And now, after a sandwich, I'm pacing on, accompanied by the gentle sound of leather boots chafing on loose rocks. It is just as good as Alpine scenery, even if it's on a smaller scale. West was an early advocate of the 'staycation'. In the introduction to his *Guide to the Lakes* West makes a rather noble plea to the 18th century easyJet brigade: "Those who make the continental tour should begin here... our northern mountains are not inferior in beauty of line or variety of summit, number of lakes and transparency of water; not in colouring of rock or softness of turf but in height and extent only."

And you sense that he might have been ripped-off by a few Alpine travel agents, for he compares the citizens of Buttermere most favourably with their foreign counterparts: "No villainous *banditti* haunt the mountains; innocent people live in the dells. Every cottager is narrative of all he knows and mountain virtue and pastoral hospitality are found at every farm. This constitutes a pleasing difference betwixt travelling here and on the continent, where every inn holder is an extortioner, and *voiturin* an imposing rogue."

It's an exhilarating stroll from now on. There's Pillar and Great Gable over the other side of Ennerdale, the Helvellyn range, the two lakes below in the Buttermere valley and fantastic views of the shattered walls of Burtness Comb on the walk to High Stile. And now spectacular glimpses down into the ravaged inclines of Eagle Crag, with eerily eroded rocks and chimneys cascading into the depths.

You get to think on these silent high-level yomps. My job started off with typewriters, moved on to computers. Now newsprint and books, the very substance of my working life, are apparently about to be outpaced by the download and Kindle. Will we soon be employing artificial intelligence to walk in the fells for us? The software of our lives changes as our personal software needs ever more upgrading. Maybe I should book another visit to my osteopath. It's more ache district than Lake District sometimes.

But concentrate on the moment and all mid-life cares are washed away. Especially when you've got a lunch in your backpack of crisps and a cheese and onion pasty.

It's a fine stroll to High Stile and then I follow the line of rusting fence posts above Bleaberry Tarn to Red Pike. Who bothered to put a metal fence up here?

The wind picks up after a stop for reflection and an apple on Red Pike. Better get down before I become a statistic in the Cockermouth Mountain Rescue Team's Annual Report. It's a knee-jerking descent down the zig-zagging tourist path to Buttermere. Three peaks completed and a great day on the fells.

This time my legs really ache back at the youth hostel. But after a rejuvenating shower I opt for the in-hostel dinner. Normally this is a good way of meeting fellow hostellers.

We're in a dining room that faces out onto the mountains. We each have a surname at our place. Only I'm seated with Mr Competitive Walker, a man who is middle-aged but lean and fit looking, and I rapidly learn, a complete know-all. I ask him if he's been walking today. "I've been along the High Stile Range and then on to Starling Dodd and Great Borne. I thought about going over to Pillar and climbing that too..."

"Was that you I saw in a mess this morning?" he asks. It emerges he'd seen my aborted foray into Burtness Comb.

"Well, there was a path there and Wainwright said there was something called Sheepbone Rake and..." I reply.

"It was you!" he accuses.

I mention that tomorrow I plan to take the bus to Keswick. "You could walk to Keswick from here!" he exclaims, going into the details of a multi-mile yomp, not having thought that my legs might need a rest. I ask him how many miles this walk is.

"Oh I never do it in miles, I just work to a time."

He's astounded that I'm here for only two nights. "What you came all the way from London for two days? You've come to the wrong place. You should have gone to Windermere."

He's here for two weeks and also from London. "You picked the wrong week to come," he carries on. "You should have come two weeks ago."

"Is that edible?" he asks of my vegetable lasagne.

I mention that before catching the bus tomorrow I'm walking to Scale Force, the Lake District's highest waterfall. "You'll do that in ten minutes," he says dismissively.

Thomas West would surely have whacked him with a Claude Glass. After dinner I find myself alone with my friend in the reading room upstairs. I ask about his favourite youth hostel.

He mentions one in the outer Hebrides. "The Peak District might be easier for you…"

What do they know of fell-walking, whom only fell walking know? Maybe Thomas West is needed still. Mr Competitive Walker needs an aesthetic education in the picturesque. Some social skills might be useful too. Mercifully I see him depart the next morning in his four-wheel drive jeep. I'm tempted to shout that he could walk not drive to London.

Next morning, there's time to walk to Scale Force before the bus arrives to take me back to London and childcare and husbandly duties. There's a brief moment of phone reception and a text from Nicola: "So glad u made it vml gd night or gd morning Nx."

Following a man with a dog, I misread a path with cairns thinking it's the way to Starling Dodd that's marked on the OS map, and take a sodden journey over faint bracken trails by Crummock Water, then travel up by a fence to eventually join the correct path by Scale Force. It's taken an hour not ten minutes, but hey, today I'm tired, an unfit southern Apple Mac wage slave uprooted to the fells.

And it's a good spot, a foot-wide rod of water plummeting a hundred feet into the narrow pool below, all in a confined mossy gully. I'm glad it didn't take just the ten minutes like my know-all friend claimed. Think Thomas West. There's three hours till my carriage arrives so perhaps it's time to get out my Claude Glass and frame the perfect picturesque English landscape.

11. DOGGED MOUNTAINEERING

Summer 2010 — Summer 2012

The Western Fells, the Southern Fells, the Northern Fells, the Eastern Fells

Soon we have a new companion for Lake District walks — our border terrier Vulcan. Our daughters had been agitating for a dog and now enjoy cuddling him at every opportunity. When Vulcan is a one-year-old we take him to the Wasdale Head Inn; dogs are allowed in the apartments for a £5 surcharge.

Vulcan makes a fine walking companion. He raises himself on his front legs taking in the network of valleys and fields and quivering with excitement. Sometimes he appears to think that the cars travelling along distant grey ribbons of roads are squirrel-like creatures he can hunt. He doesn't get this in London parks.

We have a standard lead and an extendable lead. Vulcan is a feisty border terrier who had already disgraced himself with some nips at people who have put their heads too close to his. In London our canine companion will only come when called if there isn't a juicy chicken bone to be found in the gutter. And now he's showing great interest in sheep, so as responsible dog owners we have to keep him on his lead at all times. Some primal instinct kicks in as soon as he sees sheep. He sits upright with his tail erect and pulls at his lead as we hold him back.

"Good watch!" says my wife, as she holds Vulcan's

collar and tries to get him to sit still without whimpering at the sheep. We've been taught this technique at dog training classes, but what works in Finsbury Park is more difficult on a fellside.

Our dog proves adaptable to mountain walking though and makes it up to Kirk Fell without any problem. His short legs can scramble over rocks and he seems to enjoy the adventure. He also helps pull the girls up steep sections. We sit on top of Kirk Fell, which we can see from our apartment, admiring the rusting fence posts and the views straight down to Wasdale Head, and across to Great Gable and the Scafell giants. Vulcan begs apple cores as we eat our lunch. He's walking huge distances compared to his pavement treks and slumps exhaustedly in his basket that night.

Vulcan is proving a family success — until the sheep incident. On a rainy day we walk along the shore of Wastwater and return to the Wasdale Head Inn along a footpath behind the river. As Nell is handing the lead to Nicola the pesky dog suddenly bolts, ripping the lead from her hand. Vulcan races at warp speed towards a field of sheep. The sheep scatter in panic and Vulcan gives chase.

"VULCAAAAAN!!! You terrible dog! Come back!! Oh my God he'll be shot!" Nicola moves from anger to terror.

"What can we do?" I ask, fearing catastrophe and feeling hopeless.

"Stay with the children!" shouts Nicola.

She starts to give chase. We follow as quickly as we can.

"Will Vulcan be shot by the farmer?" asks Nell.

"No we'll get him back." I say, although privately I'm imagining a ruddy-faced farmer already pointing his shotgun at us and threatening us with agricultural implements, in a merging of *Withnail and I* and *The Texas Chainsaw Massacre*.

We jog as quickly as we can with daypacks while Nicola shows Usain Bolt-like sprinting ability. Her previous life as a horsy woman makes her a formidable opponent for misbehaving animals.

"VULCAAAAAN!!! VULCAAAAAN!!! You are in so much trouble!"

Rain starts to cascade from the heavens. Vulcan is chasing the sheep from side to side of the field but mercifully doesn't appear to be attacking them as yet, even though there are plenty of large lambs with their mothers. But now he's pursuing a panicking sheep into the river. The sheep is trapped on a small island. Vulcan has leapt across the low-lying steam on to another small grassy island and has suddenly jolted to a halt. Mercifully his lead has caught on a tree root by the bank. And now Nicola is wading into the water too. There's an almighty splashing and shouting of expletives. "Bad dog! Bad dog!" Nicola's boots and trousers are soaked as she grabs the bedraggled hound and hauls him on to the river bank.

"Well done!" I shout.

"Uuurrgh. I'm soaked! Quick! We've got to get him back before the farmer sees!" exclaims my wet wife.

We jog back to the Inn all the time expecting a farmer to emerge with a shotgun, or possibly a hand-held rocket launcher. We have become the sort of urban people with sheep-harrying dogs that we tut at on *Countryfile*. It all seems most unjust as we've never actually let him off his lead, it was all a terrible accident. What would John Craven, Ellie, Anita, Tom and Adam say? Despite his ducking Vulcan looks rather pleased with his adventure as he trots back, his lead tightly gripped. Slumping into our apartment we dump the dog, head to the bar and praise providence that we have not presided over a Herdwick sheep massacre.

Unlike West Ham, we don't lose the lead again during our stay. The only other mishap is when the girls pick up a dog poo in a black plastic bag and place it in the bushes behind the hotel, planning to collect it upon their return. It's only when we are in a taxi to Seascale that they remember they have failed to collect it. Nicola bemoans the fact that our family has contributed to wrecking the Wasdale environs, and throughout the next year she threatens to send the girls back to collect it.

We move on from Wasdale to the Llama Karma Kafé on the A66, a strange slice of Peru near Penrith. At the rear of the café is a menagerie of creatures, including the llamas. After an overnight stay we join a party of llama walkers, holding the cuddly creatures with halters. Vulcan behaves well with his long-necked friends and luckily the llamas seem docile. After the llama walk through fields to the shell of a disused church, we spend the afternoon visiting the ruins of Brougham Castle.

Next stop is a B & B at Threlkeld, thinking we're over holiday dramas. My birthday is spent at Castlerigg Stone circle. It's London 2012 at home and the capital is gripped by an Olympics feelgood factor as people talk to each other and an army of friendly volunteers offers help to anyone who stands still for a moment. So we have a quiet chuckle walking past a farm with a distinctly hostile sign reading, "do NOT ask directions to the stone circle here."

But Castlerigg is a wonderful stone temple surrounded by mountains; it's impossible to believe that it wasn't placed here out of some sense of awe. Or maybe for a Neolithic equivalent of the Rydal Show sheepdog trials.

Olympic Super Sunday sees our family soar up Blencathra. We ponder maps and decide to try Sharp Edge. I'm sure I've climbed it a few years ago and it was a scramble but not too difficult. It's only when we reach Scales Tarn and start to climb Sharp Edge that I'm not so sure. Suddenly I realise that it was Narrow Edge, which I'd climbed previously. I'm an idiot. Well they are quite similar names.

My offer to turn back and go an easier route is declined. It starts off as an adventure. Soon it proves wildly over-ambitious with two small children and a dog. Vulcan starts to look down at the drops and becomes nervous. His short legs can't cope with the scrambling so we put him in my backpack. His head pokes out, accompanied by the odd whimper. Somehow we get across the first section.

Then we come up against a massive crag of black rock. We're not sure where the path goes. We veer off to the right while Nicola explores a rock chimney. The path seems to go this way. We walk another 20 yards.

"Dad' I can't move. It's too high!" wails Lola.

"What, but I thought you were ok with heights?"

"I was pretending!"

"Don't worry, we'll stay here for a bit. Let's have a rest. Look there's plenty of space to sit down. Nell, see if the path goes any further."

Nell disappears round a bend.

"Look they're not sheer drops. There's always something to hang on to. Don't worry Lola. We're nearly there. You can do it. I'll get us to the top, somehow."

Nell doesn't come back. Where is she? There's no sound from Nicola.

"Dad, I can't move!"

'But we're supposed to stay together! Where's Nicola? Where's Nell?" The dog starts to whine in my backpack. I start to whimper and curse myself, wondering if this was how Captain Scott felt when obliteration seemed inevitable. How will I explain to Mountain Rescue that I'm on Sharp Edge with a whimpering terrier in my backpack, one vertigo-suffering daughter, one lost daughter and a wife stuck up a chimney?

After what seems an aeon of dread that Nell has become hopelessly lost or plunged into a chasm she returns, oblivious to my panic and informing me there's no path. Now I've just got to coax Lola into moving.

"Ok, Lola, I'm right with you, we'll walk back to where Nicola is."

I support the newly-traumatised Lola along the path back to where we started. Nicola is half way up her rock chimney.

"This is do-able, we can get up this way!" she says from fifty feet above us.

Please God let us escape… "Right let's go for it girls. Look there are no drops here Lola, we can put our feet on the rocks and edge up it."

Slowly we inch up the rock pipe. Edging closer to the

top we finally emerge on the plateau of Blencathra. Phew.

"Right, well done everyone, let's gather our thoughts and have lunch here."

"I'm never going up another mountain again!" complains Lola.

"I'm sorry, I thought I'd been up Sharp Edge before and it was ok. But that was Narrow Edge, actually."

"It was easy," says Nell.

The dog starts to wee on rocks, every ten yards. "That's a sign he's scared," says Nicola.

"I guess I've failed the Bear Grylls test, then? I'm an idiot for getting the edges mixed up."

We sit down for a delayed lunch and Vulcan shelters in a small gap between two rocks. I feel guilty about Lola's vertigo. She'd never shown any sign of it before. The wind picks up, but despite our near-death trauma it's inspiring. We can see ways into the mysterious northern fells and across to Skiddaw. Mercifully the path back down to Scales has no ridge-walking. Somehow we get down to boost our children's morale with a pub dinner in the Horse and Farrier while watching Mo Farah win in the Olympics.

The good thing about Vulcan is that he doesn't remember grudges. In other years he starts off walking the fells with renewed eagerness. Lola will only join us if we promise we won't be going a ridge too far. Sharp Edge has traumatised my eldest daughter and will probably cost her a fortune in therapist's bills. She makes it up a few more mountains, but a few years later when she's 17 she opts to go to sun-blanched Cyprus with her friend's family rather than enjoy wet walks and soggy rolls in the Lakes. Like the Beatles I suffer the pain of realising that she's leaving our holiday home after so many years.

At least the dog behaves well when we walk in a four-strong party, as we take Nell's friend Fernanda to Ambleside. We take it in shifts to have him as his pulling can prove annoying and also you can't use walking poles holding his lead. Vulcan can handle the footpath from Ambleside and being carried through a field with a bull as we head towards the Struggle on Kirkstone Pass. We then have a half pint at the Kirkstone Inn, followed by a scramble up the daunting rockface overlooking the pass to the top of Red Screes.

In terms of canine conquering, Vulcan has been up Ben Nevis, Snowdon and most of Lakeland's higher peaks in his eight years. He's also managed to be hospitalised after eating drugs (not ours) at the Standon Calling pop festival, but he's saving that story for his memoirs.

The only time I've taken Vulcan on a solo trip was a walk from Glenridding to Stybarrow Dodd. It wasn't easy always having to hold the lead in one hand and my pace wasn't quick enough for Vulcan's liking. But we made it up the zig-zags of the path, past the busted dam that once flooded Glenridding, and took a selfie on the summit.

He's even proved a lucky football mascot, when he accompanied me to his first ever match, watching West Ham win 2-0 at Arsenal from under the table at the Churchill Inn in Ambleside one summer.

It's always satisfying to see Vulcan curled up drowsing in his basket after a day's walking, perhaps dreaming of chasing sheep and wondering why there are no discarded fried chicken bones in the fells. Even being dunked in a river and harangued for chasing sheep at Wasdale and being carried up Sharp Edge in a backpack hasn't put him off in his dogged attempts at mountaineering. My solo trips are dogless but every year we take a family trip with our faithful terrier. He still gets excited when he sees a suitcase being packed and we walk to the tube station and a long-distance walk up north. And so does his owner.

12. THE LONELINESS OF THE LONG-DISTANCE FELL-RUNNER

It's always a slightly surreal moment on top of a summit when you see someone running past you. Throughout my years of gently walking up mountains, I've been bemused by the sight of fell-runners. What would Mr Wainwright make of them? There they go in scanty shorts and lightweight trainers jogging past me as I stop for a packet of crisps half way up the path to Great Gable. My heart races and my brow pours sweat on the upward treadmill of most mountains, so what inspires the super fit to run up the bloody things?

The chance to ask came when my friend Steve Platt took up fell running. He was just another bloke from north London whom I played five-a-side with, or so I thought. Then came the Facebook posts and sponsorship requests for increasingly superhuman yomps up mountains. While I would struggle to do a ten-mile circular walk in a day, he was planning to run for 105 miles round the Lake District. In his mid-fifties he completed all 105 miles of the Lakeland 100 fell-running race. Not once, but twice, in 2010 and 2012. Though he says he doesn't run all the way up the fells — "I power walk and scramble some of the time, but limp and crawl a lot of the time too!"

In an effort to find out why he was enjoying the loneliness of the long-distance fell-runner, I met up with

Steve at a Finsbury Park café. He tells me over an Americano that it's the hallucinations that are the worst thing when you've run a hundred miles on the fells.

"On the second night of the Lakeland 100, when your weary eyes and brain hallucinate all sorts of things, I saw someone sitting on a rock with their head in their hands a few hundred yards ahead of me," Steve recalls. "When I got to the person ahead, I had just opened my mouth to ask if they were ok. When they raised their head and looked up at me, the person turned into a cat and ran away. Another time I remember crossing the road in the middle of nowhere and I could even see a line painted on it, but it looked like a river. Even though I knew it was a road I still had to tentatively dip my feet in it thinking I was going to sink! Talk about spirits from the vasty deep. In days gone by, if you were an old miner or shepherd, you'd be convinced it was witchcraft."

The Lakeland 100 winning time is often just 16 hours. "That's ridiculously fast given that the average finishing time is about twice that and up to half the runners fail to finish each year," says Platt. "There's a whole level of fell funning that I can only watch with awe as they speed off into the distance."

The reflections of sheep's eyes are another problem. Rather than meet in a cafe, Steve jokes, "we should really meet on Black Sail Pass just after dark, approaching from different directions and trying to tell the difference between head torches and the reflections of them in sheep's eyes. I have left the correct path on more than one occasion by mistaking a sheep for a fellow night runner. Sheep eyes can do all sort of things to you on the fells at night. They seem to be visible from miles away."

One of the secrets of night running is to have a good light, says Platt. "I was bought a 750 lumens headlamp as a present, it's much better than an old-fashioned head torch. By way of comparison, a single low-beam motorbike or car headlight is only about 700 lumens. It makes fog lights seem dim and is guaranteed to light up sheep's eyes on the opposite side of the valley! You don't want anyone wearing one to look at you or they'll blind you."

I know Steve from the days when he edited the *New Statesman*. My wife and I met under his editorship. Back then he liked the odd lunchtime drink and fag, as most journalists did, and seemed an unlikely ultra-runner. But his life changed after leaving the *New Statesman*, which gave him the motivation to take up more running. Then came a spinal injury, probably obtained playing five-a-side.

"I went to stand up from the sofa and couldn't feel my left leg. The nerve was crushed but luckily it regenerated. Back then I would have been happy just walking again," he says.

It was that scare that lead him to take up marathon running and then fell-running. "I'd always done a lot of walking in hills and ground level running. The Long Distance Walkers' Association organised events and at these I noticed that some people were running. I thought I can combine both. It started off as just a good way of doing the boring bits of walks. I thought I'll try and run a bit and walk a bit and see how far I can go. If I can run a marathon on the flat, can I do it in the hills?"

Ultimately he ended up doing events like first the Lakeland 50 and then the Lakeland 100, starting and finishing in Coniston. It sticks to the lofty mountain passes rather than the summits, but still includes 22,493 feet of ascent. The race starts at 5.30pm on a Friday night. "On the Saturday you hit the second night if you're not really good, that's the point you really start hallucinating," says Steve, who completed his first Lakeland 100 in 39 hours 22 minutes and 57 seconds. Incredibly he was in his mid-fifties.

"The Lakeland 100, it's an absolute bastard," emphasises Steve. "When you've done 100 miles, those last five miles take you back over the top to Coniston. You're in a quarry going up two-foot steps that seem to have been built for giants! The amazing thing is some people do stop at that last checkpoint and drop out — to have done 100 and then drop out must be terrible.

"The place I hate most is Black Sail Pass where I have been woefully lost at night. There's a theoretical path but it gets dark after Wasdale Head. In daylight it's a scramble, but at night there is no path! The only way down is to listen for the sound of waterfalls to the right. You have to try convincing yourself there are no sheer drops."

Platt trained by running and walking the course twice before the actual event. Map reading can be difficult when exhausted so it helps to know the route. There are also brief stops to change clothing, eat and go to the loo at the checkpoints.

Platt runs with a lightweight backpack containing all weather lightweight waterproofs, water, a whistle and a compass. "I grew up in Stoke-on-Trent and the first time

I went to the Lakes I was 13 and camped by Stickle Tarn with my friend and we got soaked [This sounds rather familiar]. I quickly learned to respect the weather and that the temperature drops one degree for every 300 feet of ascent."

It must take tremendous mental fortitude to complete the Lakeland 100. Did he ever feel like quitting?

"The big part is pacing yourself and having the mental side of it right. Thinking 'I've done a marathon, only three more to go!' It's worse in hot weather. There have been times when I've felt metaphorically like I'm going to die. Then you have the argument in your head. 'Well what are going to do then -- are you just going to sit down in the mud? No-one's going to come and get you.' I guess when you've edited the *New Statesman* you can cope with anything!'"

Finishing was a tremendously proud moment. "I have never been so pleased to finish something in my life – and that includes root canal surgery at the dentist," he laughs. "The trouble is that finishing is when the real pain starts. Your body says, "Right, that's it, I'm done", and starts shutting down (no more adrenaline for you, sunshine) and stiffening up. I reckon you have an hour at most before rigor mortis sets in."

"Getting to a hotel can be as difficult as the event itself. They arrange camping for duration of the event but you have to be gone on the Sunday night. I had to rest there until I felt capable of driving and then go from Coniston to Ambleside. Then it's a race to get yourself washed and changed, fed and in bed before you can't move at all."

"I could barely walk for days afterwards, but had to be in London on the Wednesday morning (after finishing early Sunday) as I had a special presentation for my charity efforts in the Team GB HQ at the Olympic Park. The walk from Stratford station to the HQ felt like it went on forever. I got there just in time to watch Bradley Wiggins win the first gold medal for Team GB before being presented with my own (pretend gold) medal in front of the assembled athletes."

Not content with superhuman feats like the Lakeland 100, Steve has also come third in the Trans Britain race (which has two and a half legs in Lakeland and is a mere 157 miles over seven days) and the Ten Peaks, which is a run across Lakeland's top ten peaks. "On the Ten Peaks the killer is finding the checkpoints on the summits. You stick your id tag (known as a "dibber") in the checkpoints and it registers you've been there. But it's a little device the size of a mobile phone and it's usually among rocks. You can spend more time looking for those things than getting to the top. Scafell Pike is all rough rock and false summits, so it's really difficult."

He's not been seriously injured running himself, bar a massively swollen ankle, but during the Trans-Britain race he had to guide down a fellow runner: "I brought someone down who had done his ankle on Helvellyn ridge. He was in a group of people who didn't know the Lakes. Sleet was coming horizontally and I was worried he was in danger of hypothermia. I thought I've got to abandon this leg of the race to take him down by the shortest route. I got a 24-hour time penalty for my pains! The time penalty was reduced, but it still cost me third place — one reason why I did it again and came third two years later."

It all sounds agonising pushing your body to these

extremes, and I think I'll stick to gentle ambling. But Steve assures me that fell running has its highs. "Sometimes you're concentrating so much on your feet so much you might miss the view, but you can do both. When you are on the tops or in valleys and you can get into that zone there's nothing like it. The run that I love is the Helvellyn ridge, there's a stretch where you don't have to bother too much about navigating. And the Corridor Route from Scafell Pike to Great Gable is fantastic.

"When you're flying down you can feel like a mountain goat. Running down scree is ok, it's fairly solid. The year I came third in the Trans Britain race I remember coming off Helvellyn into Rydal and I passed about ten people by taking the direct route down. Usually I'm too scared of breaking an ankle, but that day I felt confident. Proper fell runners, the pace they go down is mind-boggling. You have got to have absolute concentration."

It's tiring just thinking of what Steve has done, including running 2012 miles for charity in 2012, as you do. Then he finishes his coffee and announces that he's off to pick up his grandchildren. I'll take off my Gore-Tex hood to him. Though I still don't plan to become a fell-runner.

How does he respond to people saying he's mad for doing it? "You can't disagree with that, but as Alice told the Mad Hatter, all the best people are."

13. INTIMATIONS OF MORTALITY AT THE MORTAL MAN

Summer 2014

The Far Eastern Fells, the North Western fells, the Eastern Fells

When you've carried your friend's coffin, the Lake District seems like a good place to retreat to. My mate Paul died at the age of just 55 in 2014. We'd been best friends since the sixth form at school. He had managed to drink himself to death. A few years earlier my pal Nick and myself had performed an intervention and told him he had a drink problem. It didn't work. Paul eventually spent a month in the Priory clinic, seemed to stop drinking for six months, but he never truly believed he was an alcoholic. The inevitable split came with his wife Katie.

He then became a "social drinker" again, meeting for a couple of pints at Victoria station, but never letting his friends observe the true extent of his drinking. His body couldn't take the rapid detox followed by relapse. He died while having a bath, his body poisoned by booze

Paul would have been there at school for the "is the field trip a holiday?" academic debate. In the sixth form we bonded over music, and a love of punk. Paul always appreciating the absurdities of pop posing, such as the Clash looking taciturn by railings on the Marylebone Road. We visited each other at university and confided in each other about our struggles to impress women.

After college we both escaped Essex and moved to London, where we discovered its delights together, picking up discarded vegetables in Portobello Road, visiting the Record and Tape Exchange and drinking in the Gaiety pub.

Paul was always ahead of me. He married Katie and bought a flat in Notting Hill, while I was a peripatetic renter with no proper job, at one point having to sleep on the sofa in his kitchen for six weeks. He was always good company and helped his mates out; I ended up doing his old job as an editorial assistant at the National Dairy Council after he left and put in a word. I was best man at his wedding, which involved numerous venues and wearing white tuxedos on a river boat. Paul had two daughters with Katie and ended up in Brighton, a proud homeowner and editor of a utilities magazine.

But he liked the sauce as a student and then never stopped. Slowly it all went the other way. He lost his job and their house had to be sold. His marriage ended. Like all alcoholics he always found an excuse for another drink and although caustic, he remained funny to the end. We thought he would go into a slow decline... his sudden death was such a shock.

When Nick phoned with the news it was hard to digest. I took Vulcan for a walk across Clissold Park, feeling like an automaton. How could my old friend be gone? I put Mott the Hoople's *All The Young Dudes* up on Facebook as a tribute, reminded of many a drunken evening with Paul imitating Ian Hunter, and after that, *It Ain't Easy When You Fall* from Ian Hunter's solo album.

Then Nicola and I were at his funeral at a crematorium in Brighton. As a pallbearer I felt the literal dead weight of his coffin. His parents were there, witnessing what no parent should have to see. Paul's daughters Emily and Charlotte looked so young, despite being at university. It was quite a rock'n'roll ceremony, with *Behind Blue Eyes* by The Who and *Bittersweet Symphony* by The Verve being played. I gave a speech, the one I hoped I'd never have to give, as did our old schoolmate Nick. And then Paul's coffin disappeared behind a screen.

Afterwards it was drinks in a Brighton pub. Alcohol is hard to escape, and I'm lucky I don't have that addictive gene. My old pal suffered from a terrible illness. All his old friends from university and thirty-odd years of carousing were at his funeral. Ironically, it was exactly the sort of party Paul would have loved to have been at.

It was an emotionally shattering time and I needed to get away and be alone. Four days after the funeral I took the train to Windermere, and then a taxi to the Mortal Man at Troutbeck. My driver was a friendly Hungarian who couldn't quite believe his luck in finding himself working in such a spot. The afternoon sun across verdant fields was a helpful balm.

The name of the pub seemed particularly apt. The Mortal Man was originally the White House. A pub has stood on the site since 1689. It acquired the nickname The Mortal Man because of the rhyme on the inn's sign: "Oh mortal man that lives by bread, what is it makes thy nose so red? Thou silly fool thou look'st so pale, 'Tis drinking Sally Birkett's ale." The nickname became so popular that the White House name was eventually dropped. Wordsworth, Coleridge, De Quincey and Southey had all supped here, so I was in good poetic company.

My plan was to complete the Kentmere Round, my final Wainwright circular walk. I'd made it up to Yoke and Ill Bell from Staveley the previous summer, but was prevented from going further by the lengthy four-mile lane that was the only way of walking into and out of the Kentmere valley. Now my plan was to tackle the ridge walk from another angle.

The Mortal Man is a lovely old white building, with a garden overlooking the Kirkstone Pass. There had been a local drama I discovered. A fire had gutted the roof of the only other pub in the village, the Queen's Head. Fifty people had to be evacuated in the night. That evening I walked down the road to find its smouldering walls cordoned off by tape. The next morning a local hero was chatting at the hotel reception. He said he only did what anyone would do, which was to use his quad bike to get the firefighters' hoses to a nearby beck and prevent the whole pub burning down.

I'd mapped out a series of footpaths across the Kirkstone Pass road and then up on to the Garburn Pass footpath. This worked well and soon I was walking past the church and on to the top of the Garburn Pass where the path heads off for the summit of Yoke.

The path was idiot-proof in good weather, which is my kind of walk. A white line led from summit to summit and you could clearly see the outline of the horseshoe walk around the Kentmere valley. Travelling alongside a dry stone wall I was soon on Yoke and then Ill Bell. Kentmere reservoir came into view set in a deserted valley that terminated in the abrupt masses of Harter Fell and Mardale Ill Bell. Looking back the lengthy waters of Windermere sparkled in the light. Troutbeck Tongue spread out in the valley to my left and range after range swept into the distance.

The wind felt cleansing. I thought of my old mate. Reading *NME* and *Sounds*. Of watching the Clash at the Lyceum and the reformed Sex Pistols at Finsbury Park. Late nights after work together writing our fanzine *Notes from Underground*, made from typewritten copy and Letraset headlines and photocopied illicitly at work. Plotting routes into journalism and navigating London district by district. Holding Sunday morning inquests into riotous parties. My daughter Lola said Paul dressed like a rock star when she saw him in his fifties still wearing white trousers. Our lives drifted apart a bit when he moved to Brighton and we both had children. Maybe I should have seen him more of him in those final years. We knew he was struggling. But no-one thought he'd go so suddenly.

My parents had gone, so had my aunt and uncle, but that was half-expected as they reached their seventies. This felt different. I walk on to Froswick as the mountains grew craggier and sublime grey scree slopes sweep down towards the reservoir.

Like Nick Cave, I don't believe in an interventionist God. There's surely no afterlife, otherwise my old mate would be in my ear telling me to come to a party. The atmosphere feels thin up here. Just a few miles of it. We're on a large rock spinning in space among millions of other planets. There's life out there, but maybe not as we know it, Jim. Humans and our problems are insignificant in the universe. But there's also something cathartic about being out here on the mountains where the invisible hand of nature creates such rugged beauty.

Thornthwaite Crag has a splendid fourteen-foot cairn. No-one knows who constructed it. Another walker takes a picture of me leaning against it in my black and yellow Fred Perry. Four valleys are visible from here. Paths to High Street and Mardale Ill Bell lie in front of me but I've reached the day's limit as there's no way back at the end of the horseshoe without a car. So I retrace my steps and head back down to the Mortal Man. In the bar I drink to the memory of my alcoholic old friend with a pint of Sally Birkett.

It's been difficult walking the Kentmere Round without a car, as it's not on any bus routes. But I'm setting my own rules and plan to walk it in three sections via a gap of 16 years. The next two peaks of the circular walk, Mardale Ill Bell and Harter Fell, were scaled during my High Street circular walk back in 1998. So to complete the circuit the next morning I order a taxi to Kentmere.

Kentmere is an idyllic village (though sadly without a pub or shop) with a notable 14th century fortified pele tower at Kentmere Hall, now used as a farmhouse. The climb from Green Quarter up to Shipman Knotts and Kentmere Pike is a fairly easy walk, notable for the superb view down into the isolated valley of Longsleddale from Goat Scar. Kentmere Pike is 2400 feet high and a grassy dome marked by an ordnance survey pillar. It's not the most impressive of summits but it's special to me because it means I've completed all 18 of Wainwright's circular walks listed in *Fellwalking With Wainwright*.

Each year I've completed one or two of Wainwright's favourite circular walks. Taking a taxi into the sylvan Newlands valley, starting at the white church. Walking the Newlands Round, up over Hindscarth to Dale Head, taking the big drop before High Spy and then trekking over Maiden Moor and ending going over Cat Bells, that distinctive profile so prominent from Derwent Water.

If you stand in Rothay Park at Ambleside you can see the perfect mountain horseshoe of the Fairfield Round in the distance beyond a goalpost. It's a special spot where I remember my young daughters spending an age climbing a giant boulder. The round was completed at my second attempt. A decade earlier I'd been defeated by mist and such poor visibility that after Fairfield I ended up descending to Grisedale Tarn. But this time it was a stunning promenade in the sun overlooking Thirlmere while descending Heron Pike and Nab Scar into Rydal.

Another recent highlight has been the Coledale Round, starting from Braithwaite, taking in a magnificent circuit of peaks, from the triangular top of Grisedale Pike to Hopegill Head and then the wind whipping into my skin on the superb ridge walk from Eel Crag to Sail overlooking the rocky depths and hidden valleys. Every one of Wainwright's 18 circular walks has been magnificent. Perhaps I could walk them all again, or explore the numerous other lower fells not included.

My return journey from Kentmere sees me trek over the Garburn Pass, taking in the huge erratic of Badger Rock, a vast lump of rock in the middle of a field that looks like it has been dropped by some Tolkien-esque troll. My legs ache going up the walled track but soon it's a descent towards the Kirkstone Pass and a welcome meal at the Mortal Man.

My text messages to Nicola, Lola and Nell are returned

and it's good to eat alone, feeling satisfied with my achievement. I'd arrived mourning my friend, but there's strength to be found in the fells. Nothing can bring Paul back. I'm enjoying a beer and I seem to be able to stop after a pint or two, so I'm lucky. Even if it's not great for my waistline, a good ale is one of life's pleasures.

Paul wasn't one for walking, apart from the odd family trip to the South Downs. He preferred holidays to sunnier climates and European trips where he would speak English with a French accent and hope his Franglais could be understood. Things got bad at the end though. The secret stashes of booze, the morning drinking, cashing in a pension and seeming to start a new life with a new partner, the pretence of social drinking and then a sudden tragic demise. But it can't be changed now, and as Mr Wainwright pointed out, with all life throws at us it helps to have an objective.

On my final day at the Mortal Man my target is Wansfell, a short climb up out of Troutbeck. It's a moderate fell at 1601 feet but Wansfell Pike (which isn't the actual summit) has a fantastic view over the waters of Windermere, Ambleside and the ranges beyond. It feels more like suburban garden, as there's a fence with an iron gate, a remnant of when there was a toll up here. There's quite a crowd of walkers from Ambleside enjoying their sandwiches and walking along the ridge by a stone wall to the official summit. And then I return to Troutbeck to take a taxi and a train home. The last three days have helped. I'm alive and I'm climbing and for that I should be thankful.

14. STRIDING EDGILY

Summer 2016 — Summer 2017

The Eastern Fells, the Far Eastern Fells

Travelling on the 508 bus from Penrith to Glenridding, a man in a peaked cap, whom we'll call Tom, starts stroking our dog Vulcan. "I like border terriers. How many pads do you think he has on his front paws?" We guess four and five. "Wrong. It's seven!"

Tom's a garrulous soul. He tells us there's no such thing as a Patterdale terrier when we mention the mug we bought from Patterdale post office last summer. Then he shows us where he helped build two houses at Pooley Bridge when he was a teenager. He's lived in Glenridding all his life he says, as we drive along the tree-lined shore of Ullswater. After we talk about the recent floods, he recalls watching the Aberfan disaster on TV in the 1960s. Nicola has to tell him not to play with the dog's ears. Tom asks us when we met. "1642," I quip. "The start of the English civil war," answers historian Tom, who has a fine grasp of facts even though he's says he can't read.

"There's live music in the Travellers Rest tonight and there's an organ recital in the church on Monday night. Ask him, he's the verger," he says pointing to a smiling passenger across the aisle. "We'll be there," says Nicola. We're in with the locals now.

Nicola, our daughters Lola and Nell and Lola's friend

Katy get off the bus at Glenridding, lugging our heavy suitcases and backpacks with us ready for our family holiday. The train and bus journey from London has proved too much for Vulcan. He cocks a leg and wees on my Craghopper trousers. Nicola collapses in a bout of unjustified hysteria. Lola and Nell appear equally amused. Even the bus driver is laughing.

"Bloody hell! We'll have to wash them straight away in the cottage. I bet Wordsworth's terrier didn't do that. What are you laughing at?" I snap, feeling my damp leg.

Canine urination apart, Glenridding is to me a little like Bedford Falls in *It's A Wonderful Life* — the perfect place for our holiday. We'd rented the same cottage there the previous summer, trying to put some money into the local economy after the terrible floods in the winter of 2005. We'd seen the evidence of streams that had torn away their banks on the path up to Helvellyn. In the village the stone walls of Glenridding Beck were torn away, the tourist office was inundated, the Glenridding Hotel was closed and so was the ground floor of the Catstycam outdoor wear shop. The Helvellyn Country Kitchen has graphic photos of the mud and water that flooded its interior. Most telling were the huge piles of boulders by the lake. Many tonnes of rocks cascaded down from the Helvellyn range.

But a year on the place is recovering. The Glenridding Hotel is open again with a new riverside balcony with freshly made wooden benches and a raised flood wall that doubles as outdoor seating. The local deli has re-opened and so has the tourist office.

I've got to know the area after several solo stays at the White Lion in Patterdale, which offers cheap rooms, good food and a brilliant bedroom window view of Place Fell. Patterdale and Glenridding make a fine base for exploring the underrated peaks of St Sunday Crag, Sheffield Pike and Glenridding Dodd, or just sitting by the glorious Lanty's Tarn, overlooking Ullswater.

We arrive at our trusty stone cottage nestling under Glenridding Dodd, which comes with standard Lakeland fixtures such as more cooking implements than you know what to do with and lots of dvds that would be great if we could figure out how to tune the TV to dvd mode. The kids desperately seek the wi-fi code. But dvd glitches aside it's all very homely and a garden seat allows us to birdwatch and breakfast with a view of Birkhouse Moor.

A nice touch is a copy of *The Shepherd's Life* by James Rebanks on the coffee table, with a handwritten post-it note inside saying that this was written by a local farmer. It is indeed a fascinating read, detailing Rebanks' unsatisfactory schooling in Penrith, his unlikely qualification for Oxford University, and his post-graduation return to the family farm where he discovers that like his Herdwick sheep, he is "hefted" to the landscape.

After unpacking we head up the road to the Travellers Rest, watching a buzzard riding on the thermals above us. Clouds skim across mountain ridges. We're meeting our friend Julie and her daughter Clara, former Londoners who now live near Bath and are joining us for the weekend, camping at Side Farm on the other side of the lake. "I can't believe it's so beautiful, we're right in among the peaks. This is like being in the mountains in Romania," says Julie. Who needs Romania when you have the Lakes?

It's a fine old pub, the former haunt of the lead miners who worked at Greenside mine where the Helvellyn youth hostel now is. Good karma too; last year I found a wad of ten-pound notes on the floor by the bar and, having nothing like the recidivist tendencies of William Wordsworth, handed it in. A grateful holidaymaker bought me a pint in return.

Nicola has booked a paddle-boarding session on Ullswater for herself and the teenagers for the next morning. Sauntering down to the lakeside, we meet instructor Adrian who gives a safety talk as they get wet-suited up. Looking like a team of Cat Women the black rubber-clad party paddles out onto Ullswater, first on their knees and then standing up as they gain their balance. It's a glorious setting, with the mighty Place Fell overlooking the lake and a series of *Swallows and Amazons* islands to explore.

While they paddle board I take a footpath from Patterdale to Hartsop. It's a peaceful low-level walk past stone barns and gnarled trees overlooking grazing sheep. A secluded cottage offers aromatherapy and crystal treatments. It's almost like being in Stoke Newington.

My objective is Hartsop Dodd. It looks suitably Alpine, appearing to be the pointed peak of a stand-alone mountain, though in reality it is a spur from Caudale Moor. Struggling to find any signage indicating where the path might start in Hartsop I take an alternative path to Brothers Water, dodge motors on a stretch of the Kirkstone Pass and find a footpath by the Brothers Water pub. What is a dotted line on the map is very unclear in reality. My ascent takes in a lot of bracken and stream beds and eventually it's up to a dry stone wall and the summit cairn. Time to lie back and enjoy a pie and some dried mango from Lidl.

Then it's down the heather-strewn north face of Hartsop. The path is steep and zig-zags, putting a lot of strain on my thighs and calves; walking sticks slow me down a little as boots scuff into rocks. But I stumble into the village of Hartsop and mercifully discover a bus shelter — made of stone not the flimsy glass constructions of London —with a bus due in 25 minutes, saving a three-mile walk home. Another Wainwright bagged and my legs relieved.

Back at the cottage everyone's had a great time paddle boarding and there's a barbecue in progress. Julie and Clara are here and there's also our old friend, Tom, the owner of the boathouse on Ullswater, who arrives with his partner Fiona and their daughter Laura. Over vegetable kebabs Lola and Katy loudly debate Momentum tactics while recruiting young Nell, as Tom discusses inherent sexism, racism and cultural imperialism in matters of food justice. Luckily most of the houses are holiday cottages in Low Glenridding, otherwise we might be banned from conservative Cumbria, judging by some of the pub comments I've heard about Jeremy Corbyn.

The next morning we plan a walk. The previous summer we got to love Sharman's the newsagent opposite the Glenridding Hotel. The question "Do you work here?" received the reply of "Yes, for 28 years!" The shop has a fine range of pies, which we're deprived of in the south, and we came to love its green mint chocolate slices.

But our idyllic sojourn suffers from some discontent after our walk to Angle Tarn Pikes. There's glorious sun on our walk up to Boredale Hause. We stop by the green iron Victorian seat at the start of the path and eat our Hula-Hoops. It's Katy's first mountain walk and Lola is still in near-therapy after her bad experience on Sharp Edge in 2012, though she has since been up Cadair Idris in Wales and Ben Nevis in Scotland.

But as we reach Boredale Hause a mass of black cloud descends past St Sunday Crag and down the valley opposite, looking like some creature from a Stephen King novel, enveloping all before it. The Helvellyn Range has disappeared. It's still sunny where we are though, so we sit on our Gore-Tex coats by the tumbled walls of a ruined chapel, eating our rolls and dividing up a cheese and onion pie.

"You're walking fast," says Nicola to a man descending towards Patterdale.

"Aye, I'm getting away from what's coming," he answers.

It may blow over. Julie and Clara are keen to make Angle Tarn, so we set off again. But as we round the first of many bends, the squalls come in. It's on with full waterproofs. Cloud envelops the Kirkstone Pass far below. We're getting battered now.

"I'm sure it's round the next bend," I say hopefully.

Lola and Katy take selfies of each other with their hoods pulled tight around wind ravaged hair. I tell 16-year-old Nell to put on her waterproof trousers. "I don't do that stuff," she says. Teenagers!

Eventually after what seems a mighty trek but is in fact only half a windblown hour we reach the murky outline of Angle Tarn. We can make out its series of islands, which give it a misty *Game of Thrones* charm, though not for Lola, as the rain lashes into our faces.

"Can we go back now? What is the point of this? That's it! I am never going up a mountain again!"

"But it isn't a very big mountain…" I plead, "and it was sunny when we set out!"

We retrace our steps as the rain gets heavier and the winds stronger. There must be bad family karma at Angle Tarn. It's just like our Coast to Coast walk 20 years earlier, when Nicola and I squabbled as we were battered by hail and hurricanes.

Suddenly Nell is complaining that her North Face Gore-Tex hasn't worked, her leggings are soaking and her hands are cold. "But why didn't you put your waterproof trousers on when I told you to?" I complain. Hanging back, I gently cajole her along, offering my solitary glove for her hand (Nicola has the other one). "Come on Nell, we'll be down soon."

Nicola is ahead soothing Lola, who is having a meltdown and cursing her DNA and the misfortune of being the daughter of mountain-bagging idiots. Her dad is entirely to blame for the meteorological conditions. Vulcan doesn't look happy either. Clara's wet too, and Julie's wearing the wrong boots. I take the walking pole that Nell has been using and put it in my back pack. Only ten minutes later I discover that without the ballast of my waterproofs, the pole has tipped out on to the path somewhere. I instruct a sodden Nell to stay where she is while I go back to search. But I don't want to let her out of my sight in case she really is suffering from hypothermia. I can't see it anywhere, so that's one of my prize £14 Lidl walking poles gone.

The gusts ease a little as we get off Boredale Hause, but the rain is still constant. There's no sign of the rest of the party, as they've raced ahead leaving Nell and myself to die on the fells. We stagger down the lane and look into the White Lion pub. The others are in there, waving at me. Vulcan the dog has been given a towel, which Lola is now using on her hair — when she took off her waterproof a pool of water in the hood fell over her head. A pile of saturated waterproofs lie on a stool.

"Well, that went well," I quip.

"We've ordered tea," says Nicola.

Peeling off my waterproof trousers, damp Craghoppers cling to my thighs. A pot of tea arrives. Nicola has surmised that 19-year-old Lola is hungry and food will help ease her tantrum. We order the very northern dish of chips, cheese and gravy at 4pm and it seems to work.

My Steps phone app reveals that we've only walked a couple of miles. "It felt like forever, but actually we've just done the equivalent of our old school run," says a surprised Julie.

"And at least you got a selfie," I tell Lola, who has just put a portrait of a gale-strewn Katy and herself into her screensaver.

Spirits rise a little and we then stagger back along the pavements and paths to Glenridding, where socks are wrung out, boots dried and we light the log burner. Camper Julie has brought her own collection of logs, which is mightily efficient. Our clothes dry on a rack before the flames as the bad weather sets in outside. Bad days are just as much a part of the Lakes as good ones.

We change tactics. Our holiday is salvaged for those

who feel it is a teenage wasteland by a bus trip to the commercial heart of the Lakes. The 508 bus to Windermere along the Kirkstone Pass is surely the best route in the UK. Nicola starts chatting to two retired ladies who take the bus from Penrith to Windermere and then another bus on to Grasmere for a day of shopping.

We pass through Patterdale and by Hartsop Dodd and Brothers Water. Gears judder up the incline to the Kirkstone Inn, the highest pub in Cumbria, where the tumbling rocks of Red Screes guard the top of the pass and I dream of the very palatable half of porter that I drank there last summer. And here by the wind turbines is where I took the path to Caudale Moor.

Memories are etched into these mountains. It's satisfying to recognise the ridge of the Kentmere fells to our left and recall standing by the cairn on Thornthwaite Crag in my black and yellow Fred Perry, a moment now immortalised on Facebook. It's a huge drop to the valley and a solitary dry stone wall screens our bus from an *Italian Job* scenario. We drive on past the Queens Head at Troutbeck, now rebuilt after the fire of 2014, and then it's a descent into Windermere and Bowness.

Lola, Katy and Nell are overjoyed to see the numerous cafes, chip and pasty emporiums of Bowness. While I have a coffee with Vulcan, Nicola takes the girls around The World of Beatrix Potter. The very place where one-year-old Lola bolted up the ramp and out into the street much to the terror of her dad. Perhaps she had a premonition of being taken up first Sharp Edge and then Angle Tarn Pikes as a teenager. The party emerges among a throng of Japanese and American tourists, impressed by the model work and a giant Mrs

Tiggywinkle. No-one has been put in a pie by Mr McGregor.

After baked potatoes it's an open-top bus to Grasmere. We sit upstairs dodging rogue branches. "Please keep hands, arms, legs and heads within the vehicle," says the recorded commentary, followed by the very Lakeland caveat: "To our left, provided it is not raining, you can see Windermere." We travel past what "is said to be the best bus stop in the world" at Low Wood Bay overlooking the lake. Clearly our electronic guide has never been to the bus stop beneath the railway bridges at Seven Sisters Road in Finsbury Park.

Spirits revived, we return to Glenridding and Nicola and I sample the local night life — the organ recital at St Patrick's church in Patterdale. It's a fine old church, set side on to Ullswater with smaller windows to keep out the winds and snug in the shadow of St Sunday Crag. We're part of an audience of 12 listening to Mike Town going through his repertoire of everything from *The Dam Busters* to the theme from *Star Wars* and the *Blue Danube*.

Mike finishes to polite applause. As we leave Nicola, who has just interviewed our local church organist in London, engages him in conversation about church organ stops and the cost of replacing them. We talk to his roadie, who reveals that he is a southerner too. He used to holiday on the Patterdale estate — a series of wooden cabins— as a kid and then his parents moved to Cumbria. "Now I drive the boats. Do you know the *Lady of the Lake* was 35 years old when the *Titanic* was launched?"

There's always somewhere to walk in Glenridding.

Next morning we take the ferry across Ullswater to How Town and have coffee and carrot cake in a low-ceilinged tearoom at the Howtown Hotel. Lola has decided it's ok to walk at low level and she and Katy walk round the lake to Glenridding, composing Wordsworthian poetry as they go.

Nicola, Nell and myself cross a bracken-strewn path, spot the old church by Hallin Fell and climb up Steel Knotts. We find some climbers from Northumberland searching for the summit: "Wainwright makes it sound massive, but I think that's it over there." The summit might not be Alpine, but it's impressive enough for Nell to sit astride a block and instruct her dad to take a series of iPhone pics. It's an impressive vista, with the continuous ridge of the High Street range to our left and the shapely descending contours of Beda Fell and the Nab. We descend and catch the ferry back to Glenridding, finding a boat full of a coachload of Norfolk folk on a mystery tour organised by Harrison's coaches of King's Lynn — the same trips my mum and dad used to go on.

Young Nell is keen on climbing Striding Edge again after last summer's ascent. Helvellyn by the edges is a classic climb, just as Wainwright claimed, but as a part-time London fellwalker it has taken years to achieve it. I'd thought about it while staying in Patterdale in early May the previous year, but turned back after seeing snow all along the ridge. The mountains will still be there tomorrow, as they say. Eventually we made it up in the summer of 2006.

But in August this year it's perfect. It's a great climb, and not just for the Edges. On the path up the Helvellyn youth hostel is set in a former bunkhouse amid the ruins of Greenside lead mine, a scene of man-made devastation. The mine only closed in 1962. Spoil heaps cling unsteadily to the mountain side and concrete dams abound in the stream. A separate walk up to Sheffield Pike will reveal levels, diverted water channels, the remnants of huts, a series of depleted stone reservoirs by Sticks Pass and two huge industrial bites out of Hart Side.

The path from the YHA to Helvellyn soon has us at Red Tarn, an epic amphitheatre showcasing Striding and Swirral Edges and the vertical bulk of Helvellyn rising sheer above the water. A fine place to sit on a rock and eat a sandwich by the water before thoughts turn to the challenge to come.

It's not too difficult at first, more of an exhilarating scramble up Striding Edge, while all the time we try to cope with Vulcan on his lead. The drops are not vertical, but should you fall in high winds or icy conditions you can see how people die here. There's a hairy moment as Nicola gets trapped trying to descend a ten-foot rock chimney while passing Vulcan to Nell, but we get through it. A fellow climber helps her clamber down, though she does get a whack in the face with a dog paw. At least she hasn't gone the way of Robert Dixon. A memorial plaque on the ridge records the fact that he died following the Patterdale foxhounds here in 1858.

The serrated gullies of St Sunday Crag look magnificent and the lonely verdant valley of Grisedale lies below us. Then it's up what seems an impossibly sheer rock face, legs aching, to finally stumble out on to the flat plateau of the summit.

Here we find the Gough memorial, commemorating Charles Gough, a Kendal man who died after falling from Striding Edge in 1803. Gough's dog Foxie stayed with his body for three months and was found guarding his skeleton. Wordsworth and Sir Walter Scott wrote poems about the dog's fidelity, though some cynics have asked just what the dog fed on during his vigil. We wonder if Vulcan would show such loyalty, or just depart with the first walker to offer him an apple core.

On the summit Nicola phones her mum to see how her cataract operation went — enough to have Mr Wainwright cuffing my wife round the face with his flat cap, I should imagine. But the reception is extraordinarily good so she posts an Instagram selfie of us on the summit with our dog. We sit in the walled shelter eating a Tunnock's Caramel Wafer. From here we can see a glistening Windermere and Morecambe Bay.

Then it's a new challenge descending down Swirral Edge, which has sharper rocks. "Remember to keep concentrating, most people have accidents on the way down because they get complacent," I tell my companions, who completely ignore me and just get on with it.

We finish our walk close to the edges by climbing the short path to Catstycam. It's a splendid conical mountain, properly pointed with near-vertical edges. Were it not next to Helvellyn, it would be regarded as a magnificent mountain in its own right. Its sides plummet down towards Keppel Cove with its holed dam — after it burst the reservoir in Keppel Tarn flooded Glenridding in 1927, though thankfully without fatalities.

It's a wonderful airy perch up on Catstycam. Though we have reckoned without my wife's aversion to lentil soup with cream. Our younger daughter rather ruins the Wordsworthian ambiance by being embarrassed by parental flatulence. The summit echoes to her refrain of, "It farted! Dad, tell it to stop!" Is this what Wainwright meant when he insisted you took a companion who was silent?

We descend back down to Greenside and our day is made perfect by discovering that the YHA bar will serve us Snecklifter beer and white wine a full mile before the Travellers Rest.

It's always sad to leave the Lakes, but there's one final day of post-Striding Edge recovery to be had by Tom's boathouse. We take the bus down the lake and walk a hazardous stretch of road to reach the duckboarded path to the boathouse.

Amid the trees, Tom, Fiona and Laura have constructed a mini-Glastonbury Festival. There's a trendy hammock tent hanging over the ground, attached between trees, a conventional tent, a canopy for shade, and a kettle on a stick gantry boiling above the fire pit, tended by Tom's septuagenarian dad John.

Before lunch there's work to be done. John gives me a brief course in scything and tells me about his scything course. It's all in the swinging action from the waist and a low sweeping action. I feel like the Grim Reaper. The scythe needs sharpening, but my efforts manage to literally cut a swathe through an area of grass and rather attractive yellow flowering plants. "The scythe's the limit," I suggest.

Each summer Tom's party have to clear the overgrown

vegetation. Tom's dad bought the boathouse field in the 1970s long before re-wilding was fashionable and has overseen the re-foresting and a host of bio-diversity arrive. The field now has Scots pine, sycamore, horse chestnut, alder, ash, oak, beach and rowan trees, plus hundreds of shrubs, sedges, rushes, herbs and grasses.

After a lunch of barbequed sausages in rolls we mess about on the water. Lola, Katy, Nicola and Nell prove adept at rowing and paddle boarding, to the consternation of several ducks. Vulcan gets a ride too. There's plenty of gear in the boathouse. Tom is repairing his boat, which had its hull broken in three places after the 2015 floods. The water rose almost to the boathouse roof and bashed the boat against the walls. With the bridge swept away at Pooley Bridge the area was left isolated and some thieves stole part of the boathouse roof.

Tom has converted a windsurfer into a paddleboard. At the end of the small wooden pier Nicola teaches me how to kneel on the board. Lifejacket on, paddle in hand, I set off and to my surprise discover that I can move pretty fast. My direction is haphazard though and I veer into the shallows running aground on boulders before pushing off again. Discovering that you don't have to paddle at full panic-speed I gain more manoeuvrability. My attempt at standing involves a couple of unsteady seconds wobbling before falling to my knees again. Still, it's an achievement for a 58-year-old man to be paddling in any form on Ullswater, channeling Wordsworth as a Hackney hipster. Nell takes the dog out on her board, only for her paddle to snap. Luckily Tom is on hand to row out and rescue them.

The rest of the afternoon passes lying in hammocks, taking seats by the fire, reading the *Guardian*, discussing exactly what an elevator pitch is, trying to get a title for Tom's new book, and just lying back, smelling the smoke on our clothes and gazing across the water at the boats and the High Street fells. There's the Cockpit, a stone circle up there; this landscape has always been special.

We take the last bus back to Glenridding and prepare to depart. Perhaps one day we should give it a go living here for a year — see if we can survive the winter and the rain and the lack of broadband. Though I don't think Lola will be keen. But there's nothing wrong in experiencing it as a Londoner on probation. Like millions of other visitors, we enjoy our time here and during winter nights these days sparkle.

15. AT HOME WITH THE WORDSWORTHS

Summer 2017

The Central Fells, the Eastern Fells

I t's hard to enter the vale of Grasmere and not think of Wordsworth. The village is dominated as much by the poet as by the contours of Loughrigg, the Lion and the Lamb, Seat Sandal and the Helvellyn range. His old homes of Dove Cottage and Rydal Mount had long been open to the public, but they now have a relatively new companion in another former home, Allan Bank. Re-reading *The Prelude* in the summer of 2017 it's a good time to re-explore William's property portfolio.

Wordsworth seems to have had more Lakeland homes than you can shake a stanza at. Dove Cottage is the most stereotypically poetic, the sort of white-walled slate-roofed idyllic cottage that could be advertised for a grand a week in the Cumbrian cottages brochures of today.

The Dove Cottage experience begins with the Wordsworth Museum, set in a monolithic new building made of local slate. It contains a number of portraits of Wordsworth and his fellow Lakeland poets, Coleridge Southey and de Quincey, and gives a sense of how, as with most writers, finances were always a concern. A legacy from his friend Raisley Calvert of £600 a year helped and he took a rent-free house in Dorset for three years to concentrate on writing and avoid taking McJobs. He managed to marry Mary after James Lowther, the Earl of Lonsdale, finally paid the debts he owed William's late father John for his legal work with the Lowther estate.

Downstairs there are some interactive children's areas, where my 19-year-old daughter Lola and her friend Katy forget woke politics for a minute and delight in donning Wordsworthian jackets and hats, making hand on chin poetic poses for an iPhone snap, their picture looking rather like a chat between Tom Baker and a Hackney Wick craft beer drinker.

We take our place for the guided tour of Dove Cottage, which was Wordsworth's home from December 1799 to May 1808. Twenty or so tourists stand in the reception room. It used to be a pub and that's why the first two rooms have wooden panelling and slate floors. It's dark but cosy. Above the mantelpiece is a picture of Peppa, the terrier that Sir Walter Scott gave to the Wordsworths. Apparently Scott had a bit of a dog habit, arriving with dogs and dispensing them to hosts as he travelled. Thankfully most people prefer to dispense chocolates or wine today.

A stream runs under the floor of the pantry, acting as an early fridge for the poet's food. "And this is Wordsworth's coffee grinder," says our guide, pointing out the wooden box with a metal grinding handle by the kitchen parlour's window. Coffee would have been a luxury then and it would only have been used on special occasions. But it's hard not to imagine William as a hipster barista of his time, sipping Cumbrian cappuccino with his poetic mates.

The Journals of Dorothy Wordsworth give a vivid picture of life at Dove Cottage. Dorothy cooks a lot of porridge and lamb chops for William. She studies flowers and enjoys the garden. Dorothy's life is blighted by migraines, William is often ill too. Coleridge visits and leaps over the garden gate. The trio take lengthy walks outdoors and discuss poetry and the French Revolution. De Quincey and Southey drop in. Everything is geared towards William's poetry, with Dorothy transcribing his verse and inspiring him with her description of dancing daffodils. He'd tried Cambridge, London, the Alps and revolutionary France, but here he's found his mountain mojo and a soul mate in Coleridge. His imprecations of "O Friend!" in *The Prelude* still move me.

Though you wonder what the locals made of the young abstracted poet in their midst. Tourists would have visited since the days of Thomas West's guidebooks, but even so, there couldn't have been too many ex-students and Alpine travellers with an illegitimate child in France and a strange sister relationship renting in Grasmere. You can imagine the pub talk: "Aye there goes that bloody idiot Wordsworth, hanging out with the shepherds again…"

There's a lovely anecdote recorded in *The Ballad of Dorothy Wordsworth* by Frances Wilson. While living at Alfoxden House in Somerset, William, Dorothy and Samuel Coleridge spent so much time going on long clifftop walks and looking out to sea while discussing metaphysics that the locals feared they might be anarchists spying for the French.

Really they were just a bunch of hippies, getting it together in a house in the country. When I first met my wife she was hanging out with a group of greens in Oxford, a set of intellectuals who spent a lot of time discussing climate change and carbon footprints. They played ultimate Frisbee but didn't have any time for the commercialisation and tribalism of football. In many ways Wordsworth and his set of radicals must have been quite similar.

There's also the question of just how deep was William's love for Dorothy. Modern scholars have written reams speculating about a possible incestuous relationship. They lost their mother at a young age and then their father, after which Dorothy was sent to Halifax. So they didn't know each other during childhood and when they met again, each became a kind of substitute parent for the other.

When William married Mary Hutchinson, Dorothy collapsed on the day of the wedding. Much was made of Dorothy's journal entry where she describes sleeping wearing her brother's wedding ring the night before the marriage and writes that William "blessed" her twice. Though I'd like to think that most academics are just a bit over-zealous in their interpretation and that William and Dorothy just enjoyed a particularly close bond as writers (frustrated in Dorothy's case), lovers of nature and orphans.

Whatever the truth, Dove Cottage still feels like they've just left. You can feel the darkness of overcast Lakeland days, the cosiness of sitting by the fire, the fervent discussions between the Wordsworth siblings and Coleridge, and sense how cramped it must have been once William and Mary began having children.

Upstairs Labour Party activists Lola and Katy are impressed with the socialist sentiments of Wordsworth's quote, "Men who do not wear fine clothes can feel deeply." We see his bed, his ice skates in a case and then the famous couch that is mentioned in his *Daffodils* poem.

There's not too much evidence of the three young children William and Mary raised here, though the bedroom over the buttery was a nursery and is wallpapered with yellowing copies of *The Times*, dated 1800. This was an attempt at insulation, and it also suggests the trio might have been a bit bohemian in their attitude to home decor.

Elsewhere a cabinet displays a laudanum pipe used by Coleridge, always the Keith Richards to Will's Mick Jagger. The Wordsworths left in 1808 and the following year their poet pal Thomas De Quincey rented it. In his *Confessions of an English Opium Eater* De Quincey describes chillaxing at Dove Cottage with a quart of laudanum, as you do. He upset the increasingly conventional Wordsworths by altering the house and garden and publishing a little too much detail in his essays, *Recollections of the Lake Poets*.

In the garden Wordsworth's lines of poetry are displayed by the flowerbeds, as if it's literally cultivating verse. At the top of the sloping garden is the wooden platform containing a seat with a roof, built by William and his neighbour, and making a fine 'writer's shed'. Here William, Dorothy and Mary would sit looking at the then-unencumbered view of the lake and the terraces of Loughrigg Fell.

As we sit in Dove Cottage's garden platform overlooking Grasmere, Lola and Katy wonder if Wordsworth ever went on a Snapchat streak with Coleridge. "Maybe a laudanum streak," I suggest.

An interesting postscript to the Dove Cottage story is that in the late 1880s Edmund Lee, a London businessman, bought Dove Cottage for his son, a wannabe poet and probable early trustafarian. But you can't buy poetic success through association. He failed to make it as a poet, perhaps stifled by the literary heritage all around him.

Perhaps the most interesting of Wordsworth's former homes to visit today is Allan Bank, close to Grasmere on the path to Silver How. It was rented out by the National Trust until it was badly damaged by a fire in 2011. After basic repair work it was opened to the public in 2102, complete with undecorated walls and donated furniture. It all looks fashionably distressed.

There's no collections or portraits, but the visitors can use their imaginations instead. You can make your own free cups of tea and sit in any of the rooms in comfy chairs overlooking the fantastic views of Grasmere Island and Loughrigg.

The Wordsworths lived here from 1808 to 1810. "Wordsworth had a lot of problems with the fires, the smoke kept blowing back into the rooms," explains the National Trust guide. A bit like having poor wi-fi reception today, perhaps, though it seems a tremendous home to modern eyes.

But another part of the Allan Bank story is that Wordsworth was the hero of Canon Hardwicke Rawnsley, who later moved into the house and was one of the founders of the National Trust. A video, shown in the billiard room that looks like a chapel, tells the story of his life. The wonderfully-named Hardwicke sounds an intriguing character, an Oxford graduate dubbed "the most active volcano in Europe" and "a peppery old swine" by his gardener. His tutor at Oxford was fellow Lakeland lover John Ruskin, who introduced him to social reformer Octavia Hill. While collecting rents for Hill in Soho, he was so appalled by the poverty he witnessed that he had a nervous breakdown, retreating to the Lakes to recover.

When Grasmere Island was sold off to a private landlord, Rawnsley, now the vicar at Wray, was outraged and campaigned for access, soon earning the title "defender of the Lakes". He was a successful campaigner against quarry railways that would have run through the Newlands and Ennerdale valleys.

With Octavia Hill and solicitor Robert Hunter, he founded the National Trust. It was pretty socialist stuff at the time, and when the Trust purchased Aira Force at Gowbarrow Fell in 1920 a huge crowd gathered for the opening.

The house was smaller in Wordsworth's time, but both Rawnsley and Wordsworth would have enjoyed the superb gardens, set against a series of rocky outcrops. Moss grows on tree roots and the dry stone walls. Visitors take a circular path that heads towards Victorian follies, a tunnel and a high-level stone viewing seat looking across to the Lion and the Lamb.

After Allan Bank the Wordsworths then spent two unhappy years at the Old Rectory in Grasmere. It's been demolished now, but saw the death of their children

Catherine and Thomas and an estrangement with Coleridge over his drug use (they later made up).

Rydal Mount proved a much happier home. It's an upmarket gaff, closer to Ambleside. Rydal Mount is set above St Mary's church, where Wordsworth was a warden, and opposite the grounds of the 16th Century Rydal Hall. It's the house of a man who has made it, without any of the dinginess of Dove Cottage.

In the dining room is a portrait of Robert Burns — the two poets met and shared a belief in writing about normal farming folk. The drawing room is spacious and airy with French windows looking out at the gardens, designed by the poet himself. Above the fireplace is the only known portrait of a middle-aged Dorothy Wordsworth, whose devotion so helped to inspire her brother. The adjoining library is full of learned tomes. "The library is here, the study is outside," remarked one of William's servants.

Though it was here that Wordsworth probably got too comfortable. Dora Wordsworth once described it as "Idle Mount". It was said by a friend that Wordsworth had "three wives" in Mary, Dorothy, and daughter Dora. If Dove Cottage was his punk period, fresh from walking the Alps when he should have been swotting for his finals and visiting the French revolution and fathering a child out of wedlock, Rydal Mount was his more AOR period, when the poet went mainstream.

Several rooms are locked and marked private. Wordsworth's descendants still use Rydal Mount as a very special holiday home and portraits of various family members adorn the drawing room.

On the wall of William and Mary's bedroom the visitor

finds a framed copy of Wordsworth's letter to Queen Victoria declining her offer of being Poet Laureate. William writes, "The appointment I feel, however, imposes duties on me which far advanced in life as I am I can not venture to undertake and therefore I beg to decline." In a victory for romantic slackers everywhere, the Queen replied that Wordsworth wouldn't have to write any poetry. He then accepted, dutifully not writing to order, the only poet Laureate who has got away with no workload of odes.

Every room has a fine view. You can see the waters of Windermere from Wordsworth's bedroom and the squat grandeur of Loughrigg Fell. Listening to the sound of rain falling on leaves outside Dorothy's window you sense what a great environment for cultivating high thoughts this must have been.

Most touching is Dora's room. It's a small room with a creaking wooden floor and tiny bed. Wordsworth doted on his daughter, who from the age of 18 suffered from a latent form of tuberculosis. She married when she was 37 but six years later returned to Rydal Mount to be nursed by her mother Mary. She died in 1843 when William was 77 and he was distraught, saying, "She is ever with me and will be to the last moment of my life."

Fame could not protect even the most eminent Victorians from mortality. There's something very human in the image of William and Mary, the grieving elderly couple, and Dorothy, now suffering from possible dementia, planting Dora's Field, a field of daffodils below the Rydal Mount gardens. You can still enter Dora's field via a metal gate from the church. It's bracken, brambles and trees now with a lot of traffic noise, but on the circular path it's easy to imagine William, Mary and Dorothy's sad pacing among Dora's daffodils.

As the clock ticks down to five pm and the staff look agitated, I take a quick stroll around the gardens at Rydal Mount. It has several terraces, Wordsworth's summerhouse and views of Rydal Water from the bottom of the slope. There's even a Norse mound, which used to host a bonfire at times of threat.

William Wordsworth lived at Rydal Mount for 37 years, finding contentment in the "happy gardens" until he died in 1850. Dorothy died there five years later after many years of illness. While Mary died at Rydal Mount in 1859.

My final Wordsworthian trek is to the family graves at Grasmere Church. The family plot is surrounded by a low railing but remains pleasingly simple and free of grandiose monuments. I wasn't prepared for the emotional jolt of seeing William's simple grave next to Mary and Dorothy, with Dora close alongside. A single bunch of flowers has been left on his grave. Anyone who has read *The Prelude* or *Ode: Intimations of Immortality* will feel they know the man. A slumber did his spirit seal. He was certainly prescient in concepts such as the early years of childhood creating the adult character and nature healing troubled souls.

What would he make of being next to the Wordsworth Hotel and Spa and the Wordsworth Daffodil Garden? The poet is part of a Lakeland tourist trap, yet also somehow undiluted by all the commercialisation. Wordsworth is quite a modern character, really. Today he'd be called Will, go off inter-railing, dabbling in radical politics, trying to keep Sam Coleridge off the weed and probably running new age writing workshops by Ullswater. He was, like most visitors of today, a man who loved the crags and tarns and the beauty of the fells, and also, for all his self-absorption, was a literary genius who broke down barriers and helped create the cult of nature. And now he's part of his sacred landscape.

16. SUMMIT FOR THE WEEKEND

Spring 2017 — Autumn 2017

The Central Fells, the Southern Fells

I'm waiting for my mountain. A trip to Liverpool to see John Cale celebrate the 50th anniversary of the Velvet Underground and Nico's debut album allows me to meet my former flat-mate John, a veteran of 1980s London renting, now based in Bristol. He fancies a trip to Langdale to do a Saturday's walking before he has an operation on the dodgy knee he injured in a motorbike accident many years ago.

After an enjoyable dockside gig where the likes of Alison Mosshart of the Kills and Nadine Shah interpret the Velvets' songs, and a night in a hotel listening to drunken melees as the nightclubs close, we leave Liverpool in John's car. We drive past the old dock walls and a mix of the new-build housing and derelict warehouses and on to Crosby, where we stop to view Anthony Gormley's haunting sculptures on the beach.

Then it's on down the M6 and past the *Blade Runner-like* service station at Lancaster and then past Staveley on the A591 and into Ambleside. We check in at the Gables guesthouse, where John discusses labradoodles with landlady Sharyn, who announces, "He's a real ladies' dog!" as she ruffles her dog's fur. Then it's up to the Stock Ghyll deli where there's another dog conversation about border terriers. I'm able to join in and reassure the assistant that they make good pets, even if I don't mention Vulcan's disgraceful attempt at sheep chasing in Wasdale.

Having stocked up with middle-class quiches and scotch eggs, we drive down to the Langdale valley. It's a delight not to have to wait for buses, though arriving at the New Dungeon Ghyll Hotel we have to pay £5 at the bar for a parking space in the adjoining field.

The Lake District encourages reflection in the car and we catch up with news of old friends and our families, reminiscing about house-sharing in Camberwell, that dodgy tower block in Westbourne Park, John's old cottage in Cornwall, a bit of *Likely Lads*-style discussion of old amours, our seemingly inevitable metamorphosis into becoming old gits and much more.

It starts to rain as we climb up the path by Stickle Ghyll. John wearing a luminous cycling jacket and a bandana on his head that makes him look like a character from *Pirates of the Caribbean*. My 20-year-old Gore-Tex isn't as waterproof as it once was.

"We're going to walk right up those steps and show Johnny Friendly," I quip, repeating a line from *On the Waterfront,* which seems an aptly liquid title.

We carry on up slippery stone steps but it's turning into one of those May afternoons when the rain is ceaseless and the valley below is shrouded in mist.

Once we reach Stickle Tarn we loiter briefly by the dam. John's cycling jacket is soaked and the rain has penetrated through my Gore-Tex. Pavey Ark is an ominous black and we decide to descend. John's knee suffers a little on the way down the path while I'm puffing after my first walk of the year.

Back in the car we remove wet shirts and I'm left in just a damp Craghoppers fleece over bare skin. We move on to Old Dungeon Ghyll Hotel. The bar is full but we enjoy a restorative dinner outside at a table with an umbrella shielding us from the mizzle. Then it's back to the Gables, where we stay in watching *Jaws* on TV.

The following morning my wet shirt has gone missing from the drying room. Is there a secret shirt-lifter in Ambleside intent on stealing malodorous hiking wear? "Don't worry, we'll get it back," reassures Sharyn. Rather like Ernest Shackleton, we are having to cope with unexpected adversity at every step. But Sharyn is right, my shirt is indeed returned the following day, having been mistakenly packed by a male walker's wife.

John gives me a lift to Grasmere before driving home to Bristol, while I complete two days of solo walking. I stop at Miller Howe café for an Americano and some chocolate shortcake to add to my lunch. The Beatles' *You've Got To Hide Your Love Aw*ay is playing and it must sound like perfect English folk music for the three female Japanese tourists standing in the doorway. The proprietor chats in a Brummie accent to her helper as they refill my water bottle.

Then it's off down the lane. Stopping to adjust my walking poles on a bench near Allan Bank, a woman walker says, "If you turn round that sheep looks just like a lion!" And it does a bit. Who needs Zimbabwean game reserves when you have Cumbria?

My walk goes past wind-bent juniper trees up to Silver How and then across a maze of paths across the tops, stopping for glimpses into the Langdale valley, and moving on to Blea Rigg.

"Do you mind if I join you?" asks a Lancastrian man in shorts as I rest by some white quartz stones on Blea Rigg. "I've just one Wainwright left to do, Gowbarrow Fell. There's a picture of it on the wall by my late wife. I took early retirement. I'm with my daughter, she sticks to charity walks." He then reveals that he's had both knees go, both injuries occurring on low-level walks, before showing me a large scar on his knee. People talk up here. I'm reminded of the time another walker told me of his battle with cancer on the walk to Angle Tarn. If you're on the fells then you're a friend.

The bus from Grasmere back to Ambleside reveals a different bank holiday clientele. There's a stag party of young men from Newcastle, all clad in white tennis shorts and shirts, complete with headbands. "Where are their racquets?" ask a bemused elderly couple. On the upstairs deck there's a drunken chorus of *Fools Rush In* from the tennis players.

In Ambleside there's a sign on the White Hart reading, "stag parties not welcome." There are certainly plenty of them. The chip shop has been colonised by a hen party wearing red and white hooped 'Where's Wally' t-shirts.

"Can we feel your poles?" asks one of the hens as we wait in the queue, fondling the walking poles projecting out of my daypack. Which is certainly the best offer I've had in forty years of visits to the Lakes. "What's your favourite Wainwright then?" she asks. I go through a list of Langdale Pikes, Great Gable, Scafell and more, because I'm not really sure. "My most difficult one was Wetherlam!" she declares.

My new friend tells me that they're a local hen party, though she has lived in London in Putney, but at heart she's a country girl. Somehow we get on to James Rebank's book *The Shepherd's Life*. "My grandfather was a better farmer than James Rebanks!" she insists. It's possible alcohol has been partaken. "That's a very southern order," she says of my pie and chips, minus gravy. I bid adieu to my new friends, while tightly gripping my poles.

The following day it's back to Grasmere and down Easedale Lane. My route takes me past idyllic slate cottages and then across a stream and on to the footpath, re-paved with flat beds of rocks that are rather hard on the feet. The sun is out and there are great views across to the Lion and the Lamb. I walk past a pristine stone bridge arching over the stream in the middle of a field. Several families and children are ahead of me, heading for Easedale Tarn. "We'd better wait for the Robsons," suggests one mum, making me thankful that I'm not on holiday with families who have collective surnames.

On past the tumbling white waterfalls of Sour Milk Gill, the path arrives at a landscape of rounded drumlins before gently travelling up to Easedale Tarn. The tarn was a favourite day trip for the Victorians and you can see why. It's a great place to sit and eat a cranberry and Brie baguette from the Co-op and gaze up at Tarn Crag.

The path travels on past the tarn and close to a large erratic boulder near where there's a man camped out in a red tent. My plan is to walk up to Sergeant Man and get down quickly enough to catch the last train to London. To my right there's a perfect triangular mini-mountain, which is Belles Knott, the "Matterhorn of the Lakes".

After a short detour to the hidden charms of Codale Tarn it's back up to the ridge. Is there time to make

Sergeant Man? I ask a female walker on her way down where it is and she says, "It's that round thing just past the flat piece of rock." Why do I always feel amateur when asking directions? I stumble up to the top of a conical mound and throw down sticks and pack. There's my old friend Stickle Tarn down below and all the fells stretching out beyond Langdale. Misty drizzle moves in and it feels slightly scary as the visibility declines. I retrace my steps to the cairned junction on the ridge.

On the way down I pass a Gore-Tex glad couple struggling in the rain and say, "It's not far to the top." Other climbers get an ironic, "Lovely day for it!" Having bagged Sergeant Man I feel like a guru of climbing. Then like Britain post-Brexit, it's a race to the bottom. Past the man in the tent by a misty, evocative Easedale Tarn. Feet pound on rock. Steps speed up. Rain all the way. I make the 4.30pm open-top bus by four minutes, removing my wet trousers by the bus stop next to a pop-up tent advertising a talk by writer and Lakes resident Stuart Maconie.

In Ambleside I dash to my B & B to grab my case and on the bus to Windermere station get caught in terrible gridlock, just making the 6.03 train. Slowly I dry out on the train from Oxenholme to London (this might not have been too pleasant for the person next to me) and drink a pint of Hawkshead Red from Booths to celebrate another set of Wainwrights.

A few months later I return to the Old Dungeon Ghyll Hotel for my final stay of the year. Tucked into the base of the Langdale Pikes, the hotel has a languid charm that can't have changed much in centuries. After checking in, an elderly man with a military air called Derek shows me to my room. It's refreshingly simple, having no TV, just an iron-framed bed and a bathroom down the corridor. There's no wi-fi either, but a man is coming to look at it, or so say reception. Better off without it.

I recognise the lounge as the very room where Wainwright was filmed 30 years earlier chatting to Eric Robson as he waited for the rain to clear. It's belting down again, so the guests sit on comfy old sofas waiting for a change in the weather. There's a Lakeland festival organiser, an Englishman who's emigrated to Australia saying that this Brexit is "a lot of fuss about nothing" and a couple of Americans discussing GPS navigation systems, Bill Bryson and zig-zaggy paths. Eventually the rain clears and I make my way to the top of Pike o' Blisco, where the wind is so strong it's hard to stand.

Eating my dinner in the residents' bar that night a man who looks like a retired headmaster tells me he's been up to Angle Tarn. "I had an equipment failure! This new stuff is good so it's silly to hang on to your old gear from 20 years ago." Elsewhere the discussions are very middle England, on grandmothers boiling condensed milk, rescue dogs and politicians who haven't had jobs.

My next day's trip from Dungeon Ghyll is up to Bowfell via the Climber's Traverse. The path takes a little finding but it's worth the effort. The narrow path winds along the bottom of Bowfell's numerous crags, overlooking the scree-strewn brown flanks of the Langdale Pikes across the valley. There's plenty to hold on to, though a fall here could be serious and there's no-one else on the path.

My adrenalin races looking up at the sheer cliff face of Cambridge Crags. The path heads towards the magnificent ravaged outcrop of Bowfell Buttress, a huge obstacle to progress. There seems no way out, but by a high-level stream emerging from the rockface, there's a small eroded path climbing up a chute of boulders. Soon I'm next to the Great Slab, a giant flat sheet of rock tilted at an angle towards the ridge of Bowfell. It's an exhilarating climb past the Slab before the path slowly emerges on the flatter summit of Bowfell. I might be a sedentary Londoner most of the time but for a few days, at the age of 58, I'm still a fell-walking contender.

There's still some foot work to do, as there's a trek across a rocky grassless wasteland to find the summit, for stunning views of the Scafell range and Crinkle Crags.

After a fortifying bap, it's on down to Ore Gap and up again to Esk Pike, a fine peak in its own right. The descent down to Angle Tarn is another highlight, the tarn set in the shadow of Bowfell's crags. A quick check of my map reveals that Rossett Pike is only a short detour off the path, so it's a late dash to the summit, a pinnacle gained with only a short climb, before the knee-numbing descent of the Rossett Gill path. I have to pick up pace once I reach the valley of Mickleden, as darkness is arriving at 7.30pm. But it's a glorious lonely walk past the Langdale Pikes in the gloom of impending dusk, until miraculously the tiny buildings of the Old Dungeon Ghyll Hotel come into view in the distance as night beckons.

Removing my boots by the door I stop to chat to Derek, who spends a lot of time sitting on the bench looking out towards Pike o' Blisco and The Band. He reveals that he stays at the hotel for two thirds of the year and in return for odd jobs he gets a room. He lives in Chingford, London, the rest of the time. His wife is dead and because of arthritis in his knees he can't walk the fells anymore. But he can sit and dream. There's something strangely poignant about Derek sitting here with his memories of the fells.

When I depart the next day Derek is on the bus. As it drives away he points out the packhorse bridge, "That's Middle Fell Bridge where they filmed the final scene in *Brief Encounter*." When I arrive back home, a quick look at YouTube confirms he's right — Celia Johnson and Trevor Howard share a romantic kiss on the bridge before perhaps going off for a pub dinner.

On the bus Derek stops to chat to passengers at Chapel Stile and tells me about his life in Langdale: "I've got a friend who's a psychiatrist and he said, 'Why do you go when you can't walk?' I said 'You're the psychiatrist! Where would you rather be?'"

He's right. There could be no better way of spending your final years. It might not be the most dangerous or exotic place in the world, but the Lake District is a landscape that inspires people.

This southerner might live in London but I've been coming back for forty-odd years. There's always been something new to explore, it's a gradually unfolding tapestry of green and grey. I'm just over halfway through walking the Wainwright peaks and have finished all AW's circular walks. And there's a wall chart to complete.

It's been a long journey from Stickle Tarn in 1976, from DM boots to Zamberlans and Gore-Tex. Days in the Lakes linger. There are more fells to explore and tarns full of gently lapping water to have lunch by. **And that's why, like myriad other moderate mountaineers, I shall keep returning.** It's all part of the joy of being a man about tarn.